TERRORISM AND
EMERGENCY MANAGEMENT

PUBLIC ADMINISTRATION AND PUBLIC POLICY

A Comprehensive Publication Program

Executive Editor

JACK RABIN
Professor of Public Administration and Public Policy
Division of Public Affairs
The Capital College
The Pennsylvania State University–Harrisburg
Middletown, Pennsylvania

1. Public Administration as a Developing Discipline (in two parts), *by Robert T. Golembiewski*
2. Comparative National Policies on Health Care, *by Milton I. Roemer, M.D.*
3. Exclusionary Injustice: The Problem of Illegally Obtained Evidence, *by Steven R. Schlesinger*
4. Personnel Management in Government: Politics and Process, *by Jay M. Shafritz, Walter L. Balk, Albert C. Hyde, and David H. Rosenbloom* (out of print)
5. Organization Development in Public Administration (in two parts), *edited by Robert T. Golembiewski and William B. Eddy* (Part two out of print)
6. Public Administration: A Comparative Perspective. Second Edition, Revised and Expanded, *by Ferrel Heady*
7. Approaches to Planned Change (in two parts), *by Robert T. Golembiewski*
8. Program Evaluation at HEW (in three parts), *edited by James G. Abert*
9. The States and the Metropolis, *by Patricia S. Florestano and Vincent L. Marando*
10. Personnel Management in Government: Politics and Process. Second Edition, Revised and Expanded, *by Jay M. Shafritz, Albert C. Hyde, and David H. Rosenbloom*
11. Changing Bureaucracies: Understanding the Organization Before Selecting the Approach, *by William A. Medina*
12. Handbook on Public Budgeting and Financial Management, *edited by Jack Rabin and Thomas D. Lynch*
13. Encyclopedia of Policy Studies, *edited by Stuart S. Nagel*
14. Public Administration and Law: Bench v. Bureau in the United States, *by David H. Rosenbloom*
15. Handbook on Public Personnel Administration and Labor Relations, *edited by Jack Rabin, Thomas Vocino, W. Bartley Hildreth, and Gerald J. Miller*
16. Public Budgeting and Finance: Behavioral, Theoretical and Technical Perspectives, *edited by Robert T. Golembiewski and Jack Rabin*

17. Organizational Behavior and Public Management, *by Debra W. Stewart and G. David Garson*

18. The Politics of Terrorism. Second Edition, Revised and Expanded, *edited by Michael Stohl*

19. Handbook of Organization Management, *edited by William B. Eddy*

20. Organization Theory and Management, *edited by Thomas D. Lynch*

21. Labor Relations in the Public Sector, *by Richard C. Kearney*

22. Politics and Administration: Woodrow Wilson and American Public Administration, *edited by Jack Rabin and James S. Bowman*

23. Making and Managing Policy: Formulation, Analysis, Evaluation, *edited by G. Ronald Gilbert*

24. Public Administration: A Comparative Perspective. Third Edition, Revised, *by Ferrel Heady*

25. Decision Making in the Public Sector, *edited by Lloyd G. Nigro*

26. Managing Administration, *edited by Jack Rabin, Samuel Humes, and Brian S. Morgan*

27. Public Personnel Update, *edited by Michael Cohen and Robert T. Golembiewski*

28. State and Local Government Administration, *edited by Jack Rabin and Don Dodd*

29. Public Administration: A Bibliographic Guide to the Literature, *by Howard E. McCurdy*

30. Personnel Management in Government: Politics and Process. Third Edition, Revised and Expanded, *by Jay M. Shafritz, Albert C. Hyde, and David H. Rosenbloom*

31. Handbook of Information Resource Management, *edited by Jack Rabin and Edward M. Jackowski*

32. Public Administration in Developed Democracies: A Comparative Study, *edited by Donald C. Rowat*

33. The Politics of Terrorism. Third Edition, Revised and Expanded, *edited by Michael Stohl*

34. Handbook on Human Services Administration, *edited by Jack Rabin and Marcia B. Steinhauer*

35. Handbook of Public Administration, *edited by Jack Rabin, W. Bartley Hildreth, and Gerald J. Miller*

36. Ethics for Bureaucrats: An Essay on Law and Values. Second Edition, Revised and Expanded, *by John A. Rohr*

37. The Guide to the Foundations of Public Administration, *Daniel W. Martin*

38. Handbook of Strategic Management, *edited by Jack Rabin, Gerald J. Miller, and W. Bartley Hildreth*

39. Terrorism and Emergency Management: Policy and Administration, *by William L. Waugh, Jr.*

40. Organizational Behavior and Public Management. Second Edition, Revised and Expanded, *by Michael L. Vasu, Debra W. Stewart, and G. David Garson*

Other volumes in preparation

Handbook of Comparative and Development Public Administration, *edited by Ali Farazmand*

TERRORISM AND EMERGENCY MANAGEMENT

POLICY AND ADMINISTRATION

William L. Waugh, Jr.
Institute of Public Administration
Georgia State University
Atlanta, Georgia

MARCEL DEKKER, INC. • NEW YORK AND BASEL

ISBN: 0-8247-8333-6

This book is printed on acid-free paper.

MARCEL DEKKER, INC.
270 Madison Avenue, New York, New York 10016

Current printing (last digit):
10 9 8 7 6 5 4 3 2 1

PRINTED IN THE UNITED STATES OF AMERICA

PREFACE

The thesis of this book is that terrorist violence can cause catastrophic destruction on a level comparable to that caused by major natural and technological disasters. Indeed, the destruction may be more than similar when terrorists use chemical, biological, or radiological weapons or their violence results in structural failures, widespread power outages, or disruption of communication or transportation networks. For these reasons, the problem of terrorism may be best addressed in a broader fashion than is now common. In short, the emergency management model may provide a framework that will encourage such a broad view and suggest a wide range of policy options.

To the extent that analysts and policymakers are very much concerned about the potential for terrorists to inflict catastrophic damage, the timing of this analysis may be right for a reexamination of antiterrorism policies. The literature on terrorist violence certainly reflects a renewed interest in nuclear terrorism and a growing concern about terrorism as an instrument of international conflict, much more economical than conventional warfare and more practical than nuclear warfare. So-called narco-terrorism, too, is generating fears. If the analysts are to be believed, the threat of terrorism is stronger now than it has ever been. Therefore, the need for comprehensive and effective programs to lessen the risk and manage the disasters that do occur is greater than it has ever been.

In many ways, this analysis suggests that the potential for large-scale terrorism is too great to trust our response to agencies with limited views of its nature and limited resources with which to respond. Law enforcement and military concerns with apprehension of the terrorists may be secondary to disaster response and recovery efforts in the wake of a major terrorist-sponsored disaster. Moreover, an overemphasis on police and military counterterrorism operations may lessen attention to broader disaster preparedness and mitigation programs. What is suggested here is that an emergency management agency, but not necessarily the Federal Emergency Management Agency, be entrusted with lead responsibility for antiterrorism programs.

The idea for the book grew out of earlier analyses of antiterrorism policies and was given shape during a program sponsored by the Federal Emergency Management Agency and the National Association for Schools of Public Affairs and Administration during the summer of 1984. The program was designed to give a group of public administration faculty drawn from across the U.S. an overview of the emergency management function and the operations of FEMA. To date, that program has resulted in at least six books and numerous articles, book chapters, and reports on various aspects of emergency management. It is hoped that this effort will contribute to the academic and practitioner dialogues on emergency management.

William L. Waugh, Jr.
Atlanta, Georgia

CONTENTS

Preface   iii

Chapter 1
Introduction to Terrorism and Emergency Management   1

Terrorist Events as Man-Made Disasters   3
Overview of Emergency Management   4
Implications for Managing Terrorist Events   9
Overview of the Book   10
References   12

Chapter 2
The Emergency Management Policy Model   15

Introduction: The Emergency Management Function   15
Obstacles to Effective Emergency Management   18
Emergency Management Policymaking   24
Comprehensive Emergency Management   29
Conclusions: The Reality of Emergency Management   32
References   38

Chapter 3
The Terrorism Process and Antiterrorism Policy   41

    Introduction   41
    The Nature of Terrorist Violence   42
    The Process of Terrorism   52
    Theories of Response   59
    Intervening in the Process of Terrorism   62
    Managing Terrorist Events: The Challenge   68
    References   69

Chapter 4
Integrating the Policy Models   73

    A Comprehensive Emergency Management Model for
      Terrorism   74
    Mitigation of Terrorist Violence   75
    Preparedness for Terrorist Violence and Disasters   82
    Responding to Terrorist Events   86
    Recovering from Terrorist-Sponsored Disasters   89
    Conclusions: The Need for a Comprehensive Emergency
      Management Program for Terrorist-Sponsored Disasters   91
    References   93

Chapter 5
Terrorism Policies and Programs in the U.S.   97

    Introduction   97
    Defining Terrorism   102
    The Organizational Framework   104
    The Models of Terrorism and American Policy   111
    Intervening in the Terrorism Process   114
    Conclusions: The Emergency Management Model and
      American Policy   130
    References   134

Chapter 6
Managing Terrorism: Some Conclusions and
Recommendations   141

    Terrorism and the Emergency Management Perspective   144
    The Models of Terrorism and Policymaking   146
    An Emergency Management Framework for
      Antiterrorism Programs   148

Designing an Effective Emergency Management
    Mechanism   150
    References   154

Appendix
Executive Order 12656, Assignment of Emergency
Preparedness Responsibilities, November 18, 1988   157

Selected Bibliography   197

Index   209

TERRORISM AND
EMERGENCY MANAGEMENT

Chapter 1

INTRODUCTION TO TERRORISM AND EMERGENCY MANAGEMENT

Terroristic violence is not a new phenomenon; indeed, it has been a common occurrance throughout history. Since World War II, however, the tactic has assumed an importance that it has not enjoyed in its earlier incarnations. The primary reasons for that increased importance have been the amplification effect provided by modern communications media and the tremendous increases in the destructive capabilities of even very small weapons in the hands of terrorists. Seemingly minor acts of violence can have far-reaching effects. Thus, terrorism has become a very familiar tool of political conflict. In more recent years, terrorists have also demonstrated that almost anyone can become a victim and that contemporary weapons can greatly increase the number of casualties. The potential for terrorist violence, even mass casualty and mass destruction events, presents a significant risk for virtually everyone in the world, in other words.

To the extent that terrorism has become commonplace and will persist, the management of terrorist events and the resultant effects is of paramount importance. Up to this point we have been

lucky that major incidents have not produced large-scale disasters. That is not to say, however, that terrorists have not
considered or threatened catastrophic violence. Threats have been
made. Fortunately, those issuing the threats have either not
chosen to follow through with their threats or have been stopped
before they could follow through. Others have used the threats
alone to achieve political ends. Nonetheless, given that modern
industrial societies present innumerable opportunities for terroristic disruption and that terrorist organizations certainly have the
capacity for such violence, the potential for nuclear, biological,and
other forms of intentional, man-made disaster cannot be denied.
The management of that risk may perhaps be the best that can be
expected.

Terrorists need very little technological sophistication to
disrupt electrical power generating and transmitting networks,
poison municipal water supplies, destroy bridges or dams, sever
train lines and highways, and so on. Chemical, biological, and
radiological contamination is also relatively easy to accomplish.
One expert suggests that chemical and biological attacks may be
the most likely manifestation of mass destruction terrorism that
the U.S. will have to deal with in the next several decades (Jenkins,
1987). The poisoning of Israeli fruit sold in Western Europe in the
mid-1970s, the poisoning of over-the-counter medicines in the
U.S., and the threatened dioxin gas attack in Cyprus in 1987 attest
to the potential destructiveness of relatively simple acts.

The risk is real and the record is not encouraging. The spread
of terrorist violence is amply demonstrated by the number of
international terrorist incidents, the geographic spread of terroristic violence, and the increasing number of terrorist organizations (Jenkins, 1987). Increased use of repressive violence, terrorism practiced by governments and/or their agents against their
own citizens, has also been noted. Dependable statistics are hard
to find because of the ambiguous nature of the label "terrorist."
Repressive terror is particularly difficult to measure because
incumbent authorities generally control the news media and
exercise considerable control over the events in terms of being
able to structure public perceptions of their nature. That is less of

a problem when the violence is a tactic of those attempting to influence the policies of incumbent elites or to remove particular authorities, whether their objectives are as grandiose as the downfall of the regime or as restricted as a single policy change.

The statistics on acts of international terrorism, too, may be suspect. The U.S. and Western European nations, for example, routinely label hijackers of Western commercial airplanes as "terrorist" but will accept hijackers of Eastern European airplanes or Cuban boats as refugees. The point is simply that "one man's terrorist is another man's freedom fighter" (or refugee). The cliché is all important in understanding terrorism and managing terrorist events.

Todate, however, terrorist violence has largely been low scale, low intensity. There have been few cases outside of conventional war that have resulted in massive destruction and mass casualties. To the extent that there is a possibility for such large-scale destruction, there is a need to consider the consequences and to develop strategies to prepare for, mitigate the effects of, respond to, and recover from the possible events.

TERRORIST EVENTS AS MAN-MADE DISASTERS

The very vulnerability of modern societies to disruptive violence suggests that measures to manage terrorist events should be implemented if they are not already in place. The fragility of modern power, transportation, communications, and water networks and the damage that would result from their interruption demands preparation to respond to the possibility of terrorism as it does preparation for other kinds of disasters. The means to mass destruction are easily available, although few terrorist organizations have chosen to use them, and all potential targets cannot be protected. The attraction of terrorism as a tactic of political and criminal groups, as well as individuals acting alone, is manifest. The conduct of a terrorist act requires minimal technical skill, manpower, weapons, and expense, particularly if escape is not a concern of the terrorists. It is the natural tactic for weak political groups opposing a government and for persons acting in defense of government policies or authorities, whether officially or unofficially.

Without dwelling excessively on the potential for terrorism-related disasters, one can easily imagine the impact of bombings of major buildings, dams, electrical power generators, and transportation centers. We have experienced major disasters affecting those kinds of facilities and have reasonable estimates of the kinds of damage to expect and the resources necessary to respond to and recover from such disasters. We can even imagine the kind of damage that may occur with a major nuclear facility disaster, whether caused by an earthquake, a structural failure, a "normal accident," or a terrorist bomb. The events in Chernobyl, while not entirely clear, have provided an important lesson, just as the Hiroshima and Nagasaki bombings provide some guidance concerning what to expect following a nuclear bombing even though the magnitude of those explosions would be dwarfed by the destructiveness of modern nuclear weapons. What is less easily imagined is the kind of damage that might result from a biological attack or a poisoned water supply, because experience does not extend to those kinds of terrorist-sponsored disasters. What is clear, however, is that terrorism can potentially cause destruction, property damage, and human casualties, on a scale equal to that caused by major natural and other man-made disasters.

OVERVIEW OF EMERGENCY MANAGEMENT

Emergency management and disaster preparedness agencies in the U.S. are generally utilizing a four-phase model that includes the processes of preparing for, mitigating the effects of, responding to, and recovering from natural and man-made disasters (see, for example: Petak, 1985). The Federal Emergency Management Agency is promoting an Integrated Emergency Management System (IEMS) that is based on the premise that the same processes can used to deal with earthquakes and other major types of disasters. In large measure the intent has been to create emergency management capabilities that will prove equally effective in responding to natural and man-made disasters and to the conditions that would exist in the aftermath of a nuclear war. The civil defense focus of the federal programs has been controversial and will be dealt with later. The generic emergency management model is the primary concern here.

In the simplest terms, emergency or disaster preparedness involves the development of plans to respond to and reduce damage caused by a disaster. Preparedness largely involves disaster planning, including the identification of available resources for disaster response, development of interagency and interjurisdictional response accords, the training of disaster responders, and the testing of response plans (Waugh, 1988). Disaster mitigation efforts include identifying hazards and assessing levels of risk and designing programs that will reduce the level of risk. Mitigation programs seek to reduce property loss and human casualties that might result from a disaster. Examples of disaster mitigation efforts include building code regulations that will increase the survivability of buildings in earthquakes, land use regulations and flood control programs that will reduce the amount of damage in major floods, and public facility plans that control the siting of potentially hazardous facilities (Godschalk and Brower, 1985). Disaster response is the function most commonly associated with emergency management and, as will be discussed, is the one that finds the best support in the political process. Responses include providing medical assistance to casualties; conducting search and rescue operations; and, providing immediate food, clothing, and shelter to disaster victims (Clary, 1985).

The fourth phase is that of recovery which includes the maintenance of support necessary to return normal community life support systems to minimum operating levels and the provision of services that will provide foundation for long-term recovery and reconstruction (Rubin and Barbee, 1985). Normally the long-term process of reconstructing the community and preparing for the next disaster is not considered part of the emergency management process, although reconstruction is generally a major consideration in the initial emergency management efforts.

By and large, emergency preparedness efforts do not compete well for public dollars or public attention. The identification of hazards and the assessment of risks notwithstanding, potential disasters are low salience issues in the political arena. That is particularly true when the potential disasters are of low probability, high probability but low intensity, or distant. Issue salience depends upon a history of disastrous events or a very credible prediction of imminent disaster. For example, the political salience of hurricane-related programs in Florida is increasing only after strong and persistent efforts by the state government to sensitize the population to the threat of a major hurricane. Nonetheless, there are real questions concerning the public's willingness to conform to the disaster plans that the state is developing. The problem is both the length of time since the last major hurricane in south and central Florida and the tremendous development along the coast. The regulation of building along the coasts is not a popular activity for politicians. Land use is an intensely political issue at the state and local levels. The notions of "one hundred year" floods and other low-probability disasters, moreover, do not excite public interest to assure the commitment of public funds and government energies (Waugh, 1988a).

Even when issue salience is high there is no guarantee that effective policies and programs can be designed and implemented. There are serious questions about earthquake reduction programs in California despite the sensitivity of state and local authorities and the public as a whole to the risk. The biggest problem may be the difficulty in understanding what can happen in a major earthquake. Assessments of the level of risk and predictions of imminent earthquakes do little to convey the real threat posed by a major quake. The potential intensity of such a quake is inconceivable to most residents of high-risk areas. Analysts are closely examining the Mexico City earthquake of 1986 to determine the effects on buildings and other facilities.

Designing and implementing effective emergency management programs most often present insurmountable problems for policymakers and administrators. Decisionmaking processes are fragmented vertically and horizontally. The federal system divides responsibility between the state and federal governments, and state governments do not always encourage capacity building among local governments. The unwillingness of federal authorities to assume a lead role in the development of emergency management programs has become more apparent in recent years, and the willingness of state authorities to assume the lead has also been questionable. Most disasters are localized, and local authorities are most often required to assume responsibility for emergency management programs. Local fiscal and policymaking capacity to design and support effective programs is very much in doubt (Waugh, 1988b and 1989).

Horizontal fragmentation caused by the multiplicity of state and local jurisdictions that might be involved in a disaster also causes problems for policymakers and emergency managers. Mutual assistance agreements may alleviate some of the jurisdictional confusion, but disaster responses may well create unanticipated interjurisdictional problems. Similarly, interagency conflicts may interfere with disaster planning and responses.

In terms of the federally sponsored programs, the problems that have inhibited the design and implementation of effective policies and programs have included concerns that the programmatic goals of federal policymakers may seriously conflict with state and local goals. For example, May has cited the "contamination effect" of federal civil defense efforts as a major obstacle to intergovernmental cooperation. The utility of local crisis relocation planning for civil defense is the issue (May, 1985). Dozens of communities have refused to adopt crisis relocation plans because such plans may figure in the national government's assessment of capacity to survive nuclear war and may, in fact, encourage national security decisionmakers to accept nuclear war as a viable policy option. Notwithstanding that response to federal emergency management efforts, the objectives of federal and state authorities may differ significantly.

May and Williams have identified the basic problems inherent in emergency management programs operating under "shared governance," including the constraints on effective policy design and program implementation caused by the lack of technical expertise, the scarcity of fiscal resources, and confusion concerning legislatively determined agency mandates (1986: 168; Waugh, 1988c).

Emergency management policymakers have also had to contend with a fundamental public distrust of government planning efforts, strong resistance to land use and building regulation, and a tendency for the public and policymakers to focus only on recent disasters, especially at the state and local level. Levels of risk are generally difficult to measure from a technical standpoint, as well. Cause-effect relationships are elusive, probabilities of disaster are at best rough estimates, and the potential intensities of disasters are purely a matter of conjecture. In point of fact, it is most often easier from the perspective of political leaders to wait for disasters to respond rather than to attempt to prepare for them and mitigate their effects. Relief assistance is a popular political cause, indeed most federal disaster programs began as relief or recovery programs according to May and Williams (1986). They go on to suggest that "structural" mitigation programs, e.g., building of dams and levees, were the next stage in the development of emergency management and only recently have "nonstructural" programs, e.g., land use regulation and compulsory insurance programs, gained popularity among policymakers (1986: 2). The changes in focus were largely due to increasing disaster losses caused by growing development and higher population densities in hazardous areas.

The effectiveness of emergency management policies and programs, in other words, is dependent upon numerous factors, but generally it can be stated that emergency management programs do not compete well for public monies or public attention (Waugh, 1988c).

IMPLICATIONS FOR MANAGING TERRORIST EVENTS

The fortunes of emergency management programs designed to prepare for, mitigate the effects of, respond to, and recover from terrorist-spawned disaster have been somewhat better than the general patterns above would suggest. But, those same obstacles to effective policy design and program implementation still affect antiterrorist efforts. As an issue terrorism enjoys an uncommon salience due to the very nature of the phenomenon. Terrorism feeds on public attention.

The salience of the issue is also reflected in the development of an anti-terrorism industry that has a vested interest in keeping the topic on the public agenda. In some measure the efforts of the industry to give the topic high visibility may be a case of self-fulfilling prophecy to the extent that terrorism remains a useful tactic to influence political action because it commands considerable attention. The charge that journalists may encourage the use of terrorism by their coverage of the violent events may be true, but it is equally true that the attention that political leaders give the phenomenon increases its effectiveness. That an act of violence can command the attention of the president of the United States suggests that political advantage can be gained by using the tactic.

Current interest in terrorism also assures the commitment of fiscal resources to antiterrorism programs. As we will see later, that attention tends to be colored by the policy predilections of the current administration and the ambiguous nature of the violence. Nonetheless, resources have been and continue to be committed to such programs. One of the questions to be raised here is whether the federal lead role in antiterrorism policymaking should be taken for granted. Terrorism may fall through the cracks in terms of not satisfying the requirements for federal intervention. The terrorist attacks on abortion clinics is a case in point. The violence certainly fits the usual definitions of political terrorism, but, unless bombs are used, the Federal Bureau of Investigation has adjudged that local police have jurisdiction over such attacks. Federal jurisdiction is based largely on the use of certain tactics, such as bombings, bank robberies, and kidnappings, although assistance is provided local authorities in other cases. The point is that it is not always certain who is responsible for responding to particular events and that uncertainty means that federal, state, and local authorities should be developing programs to prepare for, mitigate the effects of, and recover from terrorist-sponsored emergencies. The intent here is to provide a framework for such a concerted effort.

Other issues to be addressed include the differences in how the phenomenon may be perceived by federal, state, and local authorities and how those perceptions may color policymaking. Perceptions and interpretations of the violence may be critical to the development of effective programs.

The threat of terrorist violence is real and the risk is one borne by us all. However, the level of risk has been relatively low thus far because terrorists have either chosen not to use mass destruction, mass casualty violence or have not been able to overcome our current defenses. In any case, it is unlikely that either obstacle will contain the violence forever. It remains to be seen whether effective action will result when a major terrorist disaster occurs.

OVERVIEW OF THE BOOK

The objectives in the following analysis will be to examine the current emergency management model and to suggest how a national response to terrorist violence can be fit into that model. First, the emergency management model will be more fully defined in terms of its four principal elements: preparedness, mitigation, response, and recovery. The major barriers to effective emergency management policies and programs will be examined, as well, including the problems of determining levels of risk, dealing with fragmented government responsibility, overcoming low issue salience before disasters occur, and operating in the political environment of policymaking and program management.

Second, the analysis will deal with the phenomenon of terrorism as it has manifested itself in recent decades, including how terrorist tactics have been used by governments against their own citizens (i.e., "repressive," "state," or "official terrorism"), groups sponsored or tolerated by a government and acting to repress domestic political opposition (i.e., "domestic" and "vigilante terrorism"), substate groups attempting to overthrow their own government or effect policy changes (i.e., "domestic" and "revolutionary" or "subrevolutionary terrorism"), groups supported by a government and acting internationally (i.e., "international terrorism"), and groups acting internationally without substantial support from a government (i.e., "transnational terrorism") (Milbank, 1976). Those distinctions among types of terrorist violence and groups are the ones currently employed by the Central Intelligence Agency and other intelligence, foreign policy, and, to a lesser extent, law enforcement agencies in the United States. The terms, as will be noted later, are ambiguous and the emergency management model will not necessarily be applicable to all types of antiterrorism policies, although all may be potential causes for mass destruction, high-casualty events. The inclusion of "repressive terrorism" and "vigilante terrorism" in the discussion is important because they are frequently overlooked in the policy literature and because they may be the most common forms of terrorism in the future.

Third, policies and programs designed to prepare for, mitigate the effects of, respond to, and recover from terrorist events will be fit into the emergency management model. The issue of whether emergency management policies designed for other types of disasters, such as evacuation plans for hurricanes or mutual aid agreements among public safety agencies, may be useful in terrorist-spawned disasters will also be examined at this point.

Fourth, the task environment of the managers of terrorist events will be examined in terms of the number and perspectives of the major actors, the determination of administrative responsibility and tactical authority, and the reality of "managing" events that have considerable emotional and political content beyond the destruction itself.

Fifth, current American antiterrorism policy will be analyzed in terms of what major factors have influenced and are influencing its development, whether it fits the emergency management model, and how effective it is in fulfilling the emergency management function. The analysis will particularly focus on the unique perspective of American policymakers and how that perspective has colored the response to terroristic violence.

And, sixth, the final analysis will focus on the question of whether terrorist events can be managed effectively. The emphasis will be on the need for effective preparedness, mitigation, and response; the major impediments to effective emergency management; and, recommendations to improve current policies and programs. The Integrated Emergency Management System model that is the foundation of the Federal Emergency Management Agency's current efforts will be evaluated as a possible model around which to build antiterrorism programs.

REFERENCES

Bruce B. Clary (1985) "The Evolution and Structure of Natural Hazard Policies," *Public Administration Review* (special issue): 20-28.

David R. Godschalk and David J. Brower (1985) "Mitigation Strategies and Integrated Emergency Management," *Public Administration Review* (special issue): 64-71.

Jenkins, Brian M. (1987) "The Future Course of International Terrorism," *The Futurist*(July-August): 8-13.

Peter J. May (1985) "FEMA's Role in Emergency Management: Examining Recent Experience," *Public Administration Review* (special issue): 40-48.

Peter J. May and Walter Williams (1986) *Disaster Policy Implementation: Managing Programs Under Shared Governance* (New York: Plenum Press).

David L. Milbank (1976) *International and Transnational Terrorism: Diagnosis and Prognosis,*U.S. Central Intelligence Agency, PR 10030, April.

Alvin H. Mushkatel and Louis F. Weschler (1985) "Emergency Management and the Intergovernmental System," *Public Administration Review* (special issue): 49-56.

William J. Petak (1985) "Emergency Management: A Challenge for Public Administration," *Public Administration Review* (special issue): 3-7.

Claire B. Rubin and Daniel G. Barbee (1985) "Disaster Recovery and Hazard Mitigation: Bridging the Intergovernmental Gap," *Public Administration Review* (special issue): 57-63.

William L. Waugh, Jr. (1986) "Integrating the Policy Models of Terrorism and Emergency Management," *Policy Studies Review* 6 (November): 287-300.

William L. Waugh, Jr. (1988a) "The Hyatt Skywalk Disaster, "in *Crisis Management*,edited by Michael Charles and John Choon Kim (Springfield, Ill.: Charles C. Thomas), pp. 115-129.

William L. Waugh, Jr. (1988b) "States, Counties and the Questions of Trust and Capacity," *Publius* (Winter): 189-198.

William L. Waugh, Jr. (1988c) "Current Policy and Implementation Issues in Disaster Preparedness," in *Managing Disaster*, edited by Louise Comfort (Durham, NC: Duke University Press).

William L. Waugh, Jr. (1989) "Emergency Management and the Capacities of State and Local Governments," in *Cities and Disaster: North American Studies in Emergency Management*, edited by Richard T. Sylves and William L. Waugh, Jr. (Springfield, Ill.: Charles C. Thomas Publishers).

Chapter 2

THE EMERGENCY MANAGEMENT POLICY MODEL

INTRODUCTION: THE EMERGENCY MANAGEMENT FUNCTION

In the U.S., the emergency management function has come to be identified with the four-phase model developed by the National Governors' Association (1979). That model was proposed as a means of clarifying the process for addressing natural and man-made hazards and disasters and providing a comprehensive framework for the development of emergency management policies and programs. The model divides the emergency management function into four categories or phases:

Mitigation— Deciding what to do where a risk to the health, safety, and welfare of society has been determined to exist; and implementing a risk reduction program;

Preparedness— Developing a response plan and training first responders to save lives and reduce disaster damage, including the identification of critical resources and the development of necessary agreements among responding agencies, both within the jurisdiction and with other jurisdictions;

Response– Providing emergency aid and assistance, reducing the probability of secondary damage, and minimizing problems for recovery operations; and

Recovery– Providing immediate support during the early recovery period necessary to return vital life support systems to minimum operation levels, and continuing to provide support until the community returns to normal (Petak, 1985: 3).

Mitigation and preparedness are the pre-disaster phases, response is the mid-disaster or trans-event phase, and recovery is the immediate post-disaster phase.

In brief, the function of mitigation focuses on preventing or lessening the effects of disaster and include such activities as: designing and enforcing building codes and land use regulations to lessen the effects of disaster; implementing disaster insurance programs; and, containing hazardous materials to prevent leaks. Mitigation programs have generally been built around structural or engineering solutions, such as dams, levees, filtering plants, and emission control equipment, which tend to be very expensive. Increasingly, however, mitigation efforts have been focusing on regulatory and/or planning approaches, such as land use regulations and building codes, to reduce risk or the exposure of people and facilities to known hazards (Cigler, 1988: 49-50).

The preparedness function focuses on improving the operational capabilities for emergency response, including the development of:

1. Emergency management organization,
2. Emergency operations planning,
3. Resource management,
4. Direction and control,
5. Emergency communication,
6. Alerting and warning,
7. Emergency public information,
8. Continuity of government,
9. Shelter protection,

10. Evacuation,
11. Protective measures,
12. Emergency support services,
13. Emergency reporting,
14. Training and education, and
15. Exercises and drills (McLoughlin, 1985: 168).

Generally speaking, preparedness is viewed as disaster planning, although it involves much more in terms of the development and testing of plans and the design of response mechanisms (Waugh, 1988).

The response function includes those activities immediately preceeding, during, and right after an emergency to save lives, minimize damage to property, and/or facilitate recovery, including: emergency medical assistance; search and rescue operations; sheltering and feeding those left homeless; evacuation of threatened populations; providing information to the public concerning the disaster; protecting the population from continued threats; and, preserving public order (Lewis, 1988). The response function is what we normally think of in terms of disaster management because it is the most visible of the functions. If the mitigation and preparedness programs were effective, the response should largely consist of the implementation of the disaster plans and activation of response mechanisms with adequate adaptation to unanticipated circumstances.

Lastly, the recovery function is that which focuses on restoring vital life-support systems, including: providing temporary housing; making public utilities operational; clearing debris; providing mental health counseling to victims and emergency response personnel; and, providing counseling concerning economic assistance available to victims. Restoring the community to its original, near original, or a better condition is generally beyond the scope of emergency management, although restoration should be considered in the design of a comprehensive emergency management program. The effectiveness of recovery programs generally are determined by the severity of the disaster, the resources available for recovery, and the speed of rebuilding (LaPlante,

1988: 221-222). In the U.S., when a major catastrophe outstrips state and local resources, a state governor can request a presidential disaster declaration which makes affected businesses and private citizens eligible for low-interest business and housing loans, unemployment compensation, and other aid.

OBSTACLES TO EFFECTIVE EMERGENCY MANAGEMENT

The development of an effectively functioning complex of emergency management policies and programs to prepare for specific types of natural and man-made disasters, mitigate their effects, respond to their occurrance, and recover from their destruction requires the commitment of considerable political and economic resources. As noted in Chapter 1, however, emergency management programs generally do not compete well for scarce fiscal resources and for official and public attention. Effective emergency management programs are also very difficult to design, implement, and coordinate. The reasons for those difficulties are numerous:

1. Emergency management is a low salience issue until a disaster occurs;
2. Emergency management programs lack a strong political constituency supporting effective action;
3. There is usually very strong resistance to the kinds of regulatory actions common to disaster mitigation and hazard reduction programs, particularly when benefits are difficult to document and the economic costs may be quite high, and to the kinds of planning necessary to effective action;
4. Emergency management programs generally lack an influential administrative constituency to support greater professionalization of emergency managers and better standard-setting in the design of programs;
5. The effectiveness of emergency management policies and programs is very difficult to measure, but the costs are more readily apparent;

6. The technical complexity of emergency management programs often makes them difficult to "sell" to the public and to officials and makes it difficult to design effective programs (including little understanding of the kinds of expertise that are needed for an effective program);

7. The horizontal and vertical fragmentation of the American federal system creates jurisdictional ambiguities and problems of coordination;

8. The fiscal, administrative, and policymaking capacities of state and local governments are generally uneven, creating problems in addressing highly technical problems and providing expensive, complex, and politically volatile programs at those levels;

9. The current political climate is more supportive of decentralized fiscal, administrative, and policymaking responsibility than it is of a more centralized federal role, except in defense-related matters;

10. The current emphasis on state and local self-reliance is particularly true of fiscal responsibilities, as general revenue sharing and other federal-state and federal-local transfers have been eliminated or reduced;

11. The current economic situation in the U.S., with large federal deficits and uneven fiscal resources available at state and local levels, mitigates against large budget outlays for emergency management programs, unless large disasters create a "policy window" supportive of such programs; and,

12. The sheer diversity of hazards makes the assessment of risk and the design of emergency management programs difficult (Waugh, 1989).

To be effective emergency management programs must be in place prior to the occurrence of disasters but they seldom have high salience as an issue until after a disaster strikes. Low probability events do not carry great weight in policymaking unless the consequences are so great that they cannot be ignored.

Current concerns about legal liability arising out of failure to prepare for known hazards, however, may force public officials to pay greater attention to risks to public health and safety.

Low issue salience is difficult to overcome because of the lack of a strong political constituency supporting emergency management efforts. Indeed, there may be very strong political forces resisting attempts to regulate land use, enforce strict building codes, restrict access to potentially dangerous areas, and divert funds from more popular programs. As in any regulatory activity, there usually is very strong opposition to programs that may affect the prerogatives and profits of the business community. To the extent that state and local government emergency management programs are perceived as complementary to federal civil defense efforts, there is support for increased federal funding and technical assistance. But, that perception can also mean strong community opposition to civil defense-related or even civil defense-applicable programs. The refusal of dozens of communities to have crisis relocation or evacuation plans because of their utility for civil defense authorities, thus potentially affecting decisions regarding nuclear war, is a case in point (May, 1985). Communities have also refused to have mass evacuation and other emergency management plans in order to stop the licensing of nuclear power facilities. Such is the case with the controversy over the Seabrook Nuclear Facility in New Hampshire that has been prevented from coming on-line up by the refusal of a number of communities and the State of Massachusetts to develop the necessary emergency plans. Nonetheless, the connection of emergency management and civil defense has likely increased the attention and resources given to nondefense-related programs. Indeed, the creation of the Federal Emergency Management Agency in 1979 was principally to increase the effectiveness of civil defense (GAO, 1980, 1984a).

There is also tremendous resistance to centralized planning efforts of all sorts because such activities may impinge upon the prerogatives of local authorities and business interests. The resistance may be a manifestation of a general distrust of central authority, be it state or national, or it may be a product of a more specific concern as in the case of the communities that have opted to forego evacuation planning to avoid encouraging a nuclear war. Regardless of the reason, the American aversion to planning can have a profound impact on the effectiveness of policies and programs.

Also, there is no strong administrative constituency for emergency management, although the trend is toward greater involvement by elected officials and chief administrative officers in emergency management because of increased concern over liability for failure to respond to emergencies effectively, as well as to facilitate coordination. Nonetheless, there is no single, strong professional organization supporting the development of emergency management standards. There are several small associations of emergency managers and related officials, as well as organizations of architects, public works managers, public health professionals, applied geographers, and other professionals, who do some standard-setting in very specific program areas and/or limited geographic areas. That situation may change in time due to the efforts by the Federal Emergency Management Agency and the National Association of Schools of Public Affairs and Administration to stimulate academic interest in emergency management as a field of study and as a field for professional training and education and the increased focus on emergency management by organizations such as the American Society for Public Administration and the American Public Works Association, which have special sections on emergency management to bring together practitioners and academics. Notwithstanding those efforts, the development of a professional orientation has been slow. Indeed, the reluctance to provide adequate funding for and to invest personnel resources in emergency management programs may be traced in part to the perception that emergency managers are only a little more sophisticated than the stereotypical air raid wardens of the 1940s and 1950s. The prevalence of retired military personnel with strong civil defense orientations and little training in other areas, rightly or wrongly, perpetuates that stereotype.

Due to the low probability and relative infrequency of most disasters, it is difficult to measure the benefits of a strong emergency management program. The ultimate measure of the benefit cannot be made until a disaster occurs and even the best efforts may prove inadequate when the magnitude of catastrophies exceeds expectations. Costs, however, are much more visible to policymakers and the public.

The technical sophistication demanded of emergency management programs can also be problemmatic. Mitigating the effects of and responding to volcanic hazards, for example, are relatively simple processes and very similar to the programs designed for other kinds of hazards. Strict regulation of land use and restricted access to threatened areas are the most effective responses to volcanic hazards. Preparedness, however, is somewhat complicated by the gaps in knowledge concerning volcanic processes and the potential effect on public health. Those gaps have been filled somewhat since the eruption of Mount St. Helens in 1980, but basic research is needed if scientists are to be able to inform policymakers fully (Waugh, 1990). Similarly, acts of terrorism using biological or radiological agents will present complex technical issues for emergency managers, quite apart from the issues that the police will have to address.

Horizontal and vertical fragmentation characterizes the governmental response to disasters of all sorts (Mushkatel and Weschler, 1985; May, 1985; Waugh, 1988 and 1989). The federal structure of U.S. government results in jurisdictional ambiguities with overlapping responsibilities in some cases, sharply defined but uncoordinated responsibilities in other cases, and no clear governmental responsibilities in still other cases. This is a particularly important aspect of the management of terrorism-related emergencies as it is not always clear which level of government will have principal responsibility for terrorist events and which agency will act as the lead agency coordinating the efforts of supporting agencies. The assumption that federal authorities will have principal responsibility for antiterrorism programs will be examined more closely later, particularly in terms of the mitigation, preparedness, and recovery phases of the programs, but also including the response phase. It is sufficient now to note that state and local authorities are most likely to be the first responders and may well determine the success or failure of the disaster response. The technical expertise that those first responders can bring to bear on terrorism-related disasters is a very important consideration, in other words. Simple logic would suggest that state and local government agencies will have more expertise in managing hazards and emergencies when they have more experience. Terrorism is not a familiar hazard for most jurisdictions, although the threat of terrorism has necessitated the development of programs in many cities and states, such as the preparations for the 1984 Olympics in Los Angeles and the 1988 Democratic Convention in Atlanta (Richter and Waugh, 1986).

Fundamental changes have taken place in the intergovernmental system in the past decade in terms of the expectations concerning the roles of federal, state, and local officials. The trend has ostensibly been toward greater decentralization based on local self-reliance, but there are questions about whether authority is in fact recentralizing at the state level because few states are increasing the capacities of local governments to respond to local needs (Waugh, 1988 and 1989). What is important for emergency managers is that there is less likelihood of federal dollars to support programs and more likelihood of changing programmatic emphases for the few dollars that they do receive from Washington. From the states they can expect little expansion of taxing or borrowing authority to finance local programs, but more responsibility for administering programs.

The current economic situation also mitigates against increased fiscal resources to support new emergency management programs. While some communities have enjoyed fiscal surpluses that could be used to address natural and man-made hazards, those are the exceptions rather than the rule. Budget cuts are the more likely prospect for emergency management programs. Again, it is easier to secure funding for disaster response and recovery efforts than it is to secure funding for mitigation and preparedness programs.

The variety of types of disasters that may occur also suggests that it is difficult to design effective programs to address the problems raised by each. To the extent that multi-hazard and multi-disaster emergency management programs can be developed, jurisdictions can try to adapt programs to particular circumstances. That is no less true of terrorism-related disasters. But, the forms that terrorism can take may be a real test of the applicability of multi-hazard programs.

The obstacles to effective emergency management policymaking and program design and implementation are not insurmountable, but they have profound impacts on the task environment of emergency managers and the kinds of policies and programs we have.

Having outlined those obstacles, it must be mentioned that recovery or relief efforts fare somewhat better in the policy process. Recovery in the aftermath of a disaster does in fact have high issue salience. Administrative and political constituencies do respond with special legislation and the clarification of related policies. Peter J. May has noted that about two-thirds of the twenty-five key disaster relief laws enacted in the U.S. since 1950 have come as a result of specific disasters (1988: 244). Despite that attention to relief efforts, however, the capacities of state and local governments to respond to major disasters are questionable. The levels of assistance provided by the federal government are likely to decline rather than increase if current policies continue.

EMERGENCY MANAGEMENT POLICYMAKING

The history of emergency management programs in the U.S. is as long as the history of the nation, but the idea of developing comprehensive programs focusing on the pre- and post-disaster phases as well as the disaster response is a relatively new one. Until recent decades, federal emergency management efforts were most often ad hoc responses to very localized catastrophes. Major responsibility for disaster response and relief was given to the Red Cross and other volunteer agencies. In terms of having a comprehensive, coherent set of programs based in policy, the history is much shorter, however (Table 1). By and large, the history of comprehensive emergency management can be traced from the passage of several major disaster-related programs, most

TABLE 1 Development of Emergency Management in the United States

	Civil defense	Disaster relief	Federal preparedness	Flood insurance	Fire administration
1950	FCDA	HHFA	ODM		
1953	FCDA				
1958		OCDM			
1961	OCD/DOD		ODP		
1968				FIA/HUD	
	DCPA				
1973		FDAA/HUD	FPA/GSA		
1975					USFA/DOC
1979			FEMA		

Acronyms:
DCPA Defense Civil Preparedness Agency
DOC Department of Commerce
DOD Department of Defense
FCDA Federal Civil Defense Administration
FDAA Federal Diasaster Assistance Administration
FEMA Federal Emergency Management Agency
FIA Flood Insurance Administration
FPA Federal Preparedness Administration
GSA General Services Administration
HHFA Housing Home Finance Administration
HUD Department of Housing and Urban Development
OCD Office of Civil Defense
OCDM Office of Civil Defense and Mobilization
ODM Office of Defense Mobilization
OEP Office of Emergency Planning/
Office of Emergency Preparedness
USFA U.S. Fire Administration

Source: Federal Emergency Management Agency

notably the Flood Control Act of 1936 and the Disaster Relief Act of 1950 but including the programs under the Reconstruction Finance Corporation and other agencies during the 1930s, and the development of the civil defense preparedness system following World War II (Clary, 1985: 20; Drabek, 1987).

The war experience included programs in defense and industrial mobilization, involving massive federal interventions into the economy and broad regulatory efforts affecting basic economic and social activities. While those agencies were largely dismantled at the end of the war, U.S.-Soviet conflict increased the perception of military threat.

The Office of Civil Defense Planning was established in 1948 by the Department of Defense in response to the threat of nuclear war. The functions of that office were transferred to the National Security Resources Board (NSRB) in 1949. The NSRB had responsibility for civil defense planning only until the creation of the Federal Civil Defense Administration (FCDA) in 1950. The FCDA was originally created as a part of the Executive Office of the President but later that same year it became an independent agency and remained so until 1958 (Drabek, 1987: 31).

The Office of Defense Mobilization was created during the Korean War and in 1953 was merged with the National Security Resources Board, becoming the Office of Defense Mobilization with responsibility for all emergency preparedness programs except for civil defense. Confusion concerning agency responsibilities lead to a reorganization in 1958 which included the merger of programs under the control of a new Office of Civil Defense Mobilization located in the Executive Office of the President. A large part of the confusion was due to differences in orientation concerning the responsibilities of federal, state, and local agencies. The Federal Civil Defense Act of 1950 indicated that local governments should have primary responsibility for civil preparedness (Drabek, 1987: 32-33).

In 1961, the Office of Civil Defense was created within the Department of Defense and shared responsibilities with the Office of Civil Defense Mobilization which later became the Office of Emergency Planning and later the Office of Emergency Preparedness. The Office of Civil Defense became the Defense Civil Preparedness Agency in 1972 and the Office of Emergency Preparedness was abolished in 1973.

On the nondefense side, in the early 1970s, the Federal Preparedness Agency was established within the General Services Administration and the Federal Disaster Assistance Administration was established within the Department of Housing and Urban Development. The federal arrangements created confusion among local officials (Drabek, 1987: 33-34).

The federal role in flood-related hazard mitigation was expanded from the Army Corps of Engineers responsibilities for flood control under the Flood Control Act of 1936 with the passage of the National Flood Insurance Act in 1968. Emphasis was placed on peacetime applications of emergency management programs and local government capacity building in the early 1970's. Crisis relocation and contingency planning became the program emphases in 1974. Federal responsibilities for disaster response broadened considerably in 1977 with the passage of the Earthquake Hazards Reduction Act.

The expanding federal role in nondefense-related disaster management created a patchwork of programs that created considerable jurisdictional confusion, particularly relative to the civil defense programs. To alleviate those problems, Executive Order 12127 in 1979 created the Federal Emergency Management Agency (FEMA), consolidating responsibility for emergency management programs by bringing together the Defense Civil Preparedness Agency from the Department of Defense, the Federal Disaster Assistance Administration from the Department of Housing and Urban Development, and the Federal Preparedness Administration from the General Services Administration. Following the creation of the agency other programs were added to the list of FEMA responsibilities, including: dam safety coordination; earthquake hazard reduction; consequences management in terrorism; warning and emergency broadcast (all from the Executive Office of the President); the Federal Flood Insurance Administration (from the Department of Housing and Urban Development); the National Fire Prevention and Control Administration, including the National Fire Academy (from the Department of Commerce); and, the Community Preparedness Program (from the National Weather Service, Department of Commerce) (McLoughlin, 1985).

The newly formed agency has not been without problems, however. The effectiveness of the agency has been reduced considerably by a number of factors, some within the control of the agency and others not, including: a reticence on the part of FEMA officials to assume lead roles in some areas of emergency management, jurisdictional conflicts within the agency itself, intergovernmental conflicts between FEMA and other federal agencies and between FEMA and state and local authorities, inadequate coordination mechanisms to assure effective multi-agency responses, overlapping agency responsibilities causing duplication of efforts, charges of corruption and other irregularites involving FEMA officials, opposition to the civil defense focus of many FEMA programs, and confusion among state and local officials because of the changing programmatic priorities of the agency (GAO, 1980a, 1980b, 1983a, 1983b, 1984a, 1984b; Clary, 1985; Perry, 1985; May and Williams, 1986; Waugh, 1988 and 1989).

In terms of emergency management programs to address the hazard presented by terrorism and the potential for catastrophic events, the agency responsibilities are unclear. Later chapters will focus on the nature of such a comprehensive emergency management program and current agency responsibilities. It is sufficient to note here that there was some conflict between the Federal Emergency Management Agency and other agencies over responsibility for responding to terrorist sponsored acts. FEMA and the Nuclear Regulatory Agency were in conflict over which agency had jurisdictional responsibility for the security of nuclear facilities. That was the apparent focus of the conflict, although jurisdictional conflicts with other agencies also arose. FEMA's role in organizing international conferences on terrorism and its public role in responding to terrorist events appears to have decreased since the mid-1980s.

COMPREHENSIVE EMERGENCY MANAGEMENT

The diverse programs brought together under the Federal Emergency Management Agency, as well as the need for effective cooperation and coordination with state and local government agencies, supported the development of a more comprehensive, all-hazard approach to emergency management. The development of what is called the Integrated Emergency Management System (IEMS) also provides a vehicle for merging the emergency management programs for civil defense with those for other man-made and natural disasters. When fully implemented, it may also provide a framework for coordinating the very diverse organizational and programmatic units responsible for emergency management functions in most states and communities. The effectiveness of such an integrated system for reducing hazards presented by terrorist organizations and responding to disasters resulting from terrorist violence will be examined in some detail later.

In its simplest terms, the IEMS model suggests that programs should take the following steps (FEMA, 1983; McLoughlin, 1985):

1. Hazard Analysis – including: the identification of hazards; the determination of probability of a disaster, the likely intensity, and probable location; the assessment of potential impact on a community; the property, persons, and areas at risk; and, the assignment of priorities based on exposure.

2. Capability Assessment – including: the current emergency management organization and plan; the alert and warning system; emergency communications system; available shelter; evacuation plans; emergency medical services; and, the level of training and education among emergency personnel. The capability assessment should lead to the identification of capability shortfalls. Emergency management agencies can then develop long- and short-term plans to increase capability with attention to the available and necessary state, local, and federal resources. FEMA suggests a five-year plan with an annual development plan leading to the identification of an annual work increment.

3. Emergency Planning – including: coordinated planning efforts involving all responsible officials, not just emergency managers; planning for unique aspects of a hazard; setting capability standards against which current readiness status can be measured; and, planning for capability improvement.

4. Capability Maintenance – including: testing and updating plans; testing and servicing equipment; training and educating emergency personnel; and, educating other officials and the public.

5. Emergency response – including: putting the emergency plans into operation; identifying unanticipated consequences and adjusting the response accordingly; and, evaluating the response as soon as time permits so that formal adjustments can be made in the emergency plan and/or the organization of the response. The evaluation of the emergency response should yield information to improve the hazard analysis and the capability assessment.

6. Recovery Efforts – including: returning vital life support systems to minimum operating level as soon as possible; using the disaster experience to improve mitigation efforts and the hazard analysis; and, using the recovery experience to improve the disaster response itself.

The relationships among the components of the IEMS model are illustrated in Figure 1. The model does not imply that all disasters are alike and all emergency management functions are interchangeable, but it does suggest that the response requirements are sufficiently alike to make an integrated approach more effective than attempting to develop a large reportoire of programs, each with its own jurisdiction, organizational structure, and priorities. The objective here is not to argue for or against the model, rather it is to examine its utility when applied to hazards presented by terrorist organizations and disasters resulting from their activities.

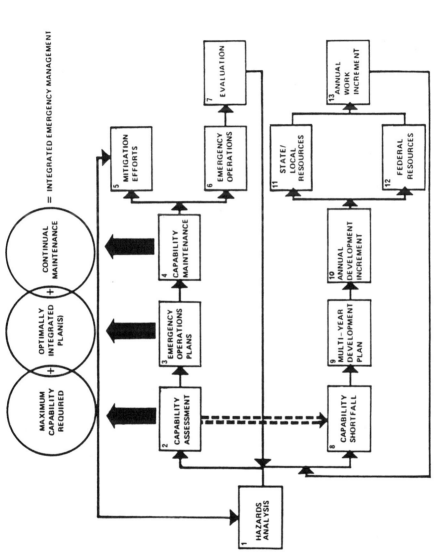

FIGURE 1 The integrated emergency management system. (From Federal Emergency Management Agency.)

CONCLUSIONS: THE REALITY OF EMERGENCY MANAGEMENT

The listing of obstacles to effective emergency management policymaking and program management is not encouraging, although there are indications that more attention is being paid to the critical issues by public officials, academic researchers, professional organizations, and other groups. That is, emergency management seems to be gaining greater recognition as a vital administrative function, as well as gaining greater political and administrative support, although financial resources are still quite scarce and efforts to regulate land use, building codes, and other activities have to overcome tremendous resistance.

Technical problems are also being addressed in terms of basic research on earthquakes and other hazards and the development of technologies with emergency management applications, e.g., decision support systems, sophisticated warning systems, and effective communication systems for emergency response personnel (Congressional Research Service, 1984).

The weakest links in emergency management, however, appear to be organizational and political. The organizational structure of emergency management is a maze of agencies ranging from the National Forest Service to the U.S. Army Corps of Engineers and from the Federal Emergency Management Agency to local hospitals and police departments. To illustrate the complexity of the emergency management organizational arrangements, Table 2 indicates the agencies responsible for responding to public health emergencies.

Once the Office of the Assistant Secretary for Health, Public Health Service (PHS), determines that a acute chemical waste emergency exists all appropriate agencies are notified by the Centers for Disease Control (CDC) with the assistance of the PHS's Office of Emergency Preparedness and the Health Resources and Services Administration. The CDC, with the support of the National Institute of Health (NIH), is responsible for collecting technical information, and, with the support of the NIH and the Food and Drug Administration (FDA), is responsible for investigating the nature and extent of the threat. The emergency

TABLE 2 Guide for Public Health Response

Response steps	Type of Incident				
	Radiation emergencies	Acute chemical emergencies	Toxic waste crisis	Air pollution emergencies	Biological emergencies
A. Decide if emergency exists	ASH	ASH	ASH	ASH	ASH
B. Notify all Appropriate PHS Components	CDC (OEP/HRSA)[a]	CDC (OEP/HRSA)	CDC (OEP/HRSA)	CDC (OEP/HRSA)	CDC (OEP/HRSA)
C. (1) Gather technical information about source	FDA (NIH)	CDC (NIH)	CDC (NIH)	CDC (NIH)	CDC (NIH)
(2) Tentatively identify and describe nature, location and extent of potential health problems	CDC (FDA/NIH)	CDC (FDA/NIH)	CDC (FDA/NIH)	CDC (FDA/NIH)	CDC (FDA/NIH)
(3) Establish and conduct appropriate surveillance to obtain ongoing information on which to base decisions	CDC/FDA	CDC/FDA/NIH HSRA	CDC/HSRA/ FDA	CDC (FDA)	CDC (FDA)
D. Reassess, decide whether to continue in crisis mode	ASH	ASH	ASH	ASH	ASH
E. Develop and implement PHS activities to protect public	CDC	CDC	CDC	CDC	CDC
(1) Determine response capacity of local community	HRSA/FDA	HRSA/FDA	HRSA/FDA	HRSA/FDA	HRSA/FDA

TABLE 2   *(continued)*

Response steps	Radiation emergencies	Acute chemical emergencies	Toxic waste crisis	Air pollution emergencies	Biological emergencies
			Type of Incident		
(2) Provide medical personnel to assist in triage/treatment	HRSA	HRSA (CDC)	HRSA (CDC)	HRSA	HRSA (CDC)
(3) Advise FEMA of need for additional health resources	HRSA	HRSA	HRSA	HRSA	HRSA
(4) Provide or assist in locating needed medical supplies	FDA (CDC)	HRSA (CDC,FDA)	HRSA (NIOSH,FDA)	HRSA (NIOSH,FDA)	FDA (CDC)
(5) Provide assistance in evacuation					
medical care[a]	HRSA	HRSA	HRSA	HRSA	HRSA
health surveillance[a]	CDC	CDC	CDC	CDC	CDC
(6) Prevent exposure via food chain and other sources	FDA	FDA	FDA	FDA	FDA

(7) Advise on protection of workers and clean-up personnel	CDC/NIOSH	CDC/NIOSH	CDC/NIOSH	CDC/NIOSH	CDC/NIOSH
(8) Provide technical assist/advice on decontamination people[a] environment[a]	FDA (CDC)	CDC/NIOSH	FDA CDC/NIOSH	FDA CDC/NIOSH	CDC/FDA
(9) Advise on funding and administer funds for crisis counseling services and mental health training materials for disaster workers	ADAMHA	ADAMHA	ADAMHA	ADAMHA	ADAMHA
(10) Assist in collection of appropriate bioligical specimens	CDC HRSA/FDA	CDC HRSA/FDA	CDC HRSA/FDA	CDC HRSA/FDA	CDC HRSA/FDA
(11) Provide health information to public via FEMA or other spokesman	CDC (FDA/HRSA)	CDC (FDA/HRSA)	CDC (FDA/HRSA)	CDC (FDA/HRSA)	CDC (FDA/HRSA)
(12) Assist in training of medical personnel	CDC (FDA,HRSA)	CDC (FDA,HRSA)	CDC (FDA,HRSA)	CDC (FDA,HRSA)	CDC (FDA,HRSA)
(13) Assist in formulating damage and casualty estimates	CDC (HRSA)	CDC (HRSA)	CDC (HRSA)	CDC (HRSA)	CDC (HRSA)

TABLE 2 (continued)

Response steps	Type of Incident				
	Radiation emergencies	Acute chemical emergencies	Toxic waste crisis	Air pollution emergencies	Biological emergencies
(14) Provide health advice to state/local officials	CDC (FDA)	CDC (FDA)	CDC (FDA)	CDC (FDA)	CDC (FDA)
(15) Prevent further spread from source	[b]	CDC (FDA)	CDC (FDA)	CDC (FDA)	CDC (FDA)
F. Decide when protection, treatment, and prevention objectives are achieved	CDC (FDA/HRSA)	CDC (FDA/HRSA)	CDC (FDA/HRSA)	CDC (FDA/HRSA)	CDC (FDA/HRSA)
G. Conduct research relating to long-term effects of exposure	CDC (NIH)	CDC (NIH)	CDC (NIH)	CDC (NIH)	CDC (NIH)
H. Conduct evaluations, issue reports with recommendations	CDC (HRSA)	CDC (HRSA)	CDC (HRSA)	CDC (HRSA)	CDC (HRSA)

[a]Lead Organizations for each activity listed first; supporting organizations in parentheses.
[b]In radiation emergencies, the radiation source will likely be under control of one or more of the following agencies: DCD, DOE, DOT, NRC.
Source: Public Health Service, Centers for Disease Control.

response itself may involve a wide variety of agencies, including the CDC, NIH, HRSA, FDA, National Institute of Occupational Safety and Health, and Alcohol, Drug Abuse, and Mental Health Administration (ADAMHA). The new Agency for Toxic Substances and Disease Registry now would assume some of the responsibilities assigned to the CDC in Table 2. Other CDC guides acknowledge that the Federal Emergency Management Agency, Environmental Protection Agency, Occupational Safety and Health Administration, Department of Transportation, and other agencies may have lead roles in acute chemical emergencies, as well (Allen, 1990). The involvement of state and local agencies would further complicate the process of responding to such an emergency. The point is that coordination can be a difficult task given the number of jurisdictions that might be involved. The development of clear lines of responsibility and effective mechanisms for the coordination of multi-agency responses are critical components of emergency management. Ambiguous organizational arrangements are a usual feature of emergency responses, rather than an unusual one.

Similarly, responsibility for designing, implementing, and operating a comprehensive emergency management program is generally shared by a number of agencies within and across jurisdictions and the capacities of those agencies to deal with complex environmental and technological problems varies tremendously. Confusion over which agencies and levels of government should have lead roles in particular disasters or in response to particular hazards, as well as controversy over which should assume principal responsibility for funding and administering programs, still confounds the process of capacity-building.

The historical development of emergency management programs, moreover, has not resolved the confusion over jurisdictions and responsibilities. There is, however, a better understanding of the function of emergency management and the need for coordination, as is evident in the development of the Integrated Emergency Management System. In large measure, the problems that have been and will be encountered in the design and implementation of programs to mitigate, prepare for, respond to, and recover from terrorism-related hazards and disasters are the same as those experienced with other types of hazards. As will be seen in the following analyses, however, terrorism may present new problems of perception or hazard identification, risk assessment, and interjurisdictional coordination of emergency management efforts.

REFERENCES

Caffilene Allen (1990) "Public Health Hazards and Emergencies," in *Emergency Management Handbook*, edited by William L. Waugh, Jr., and Ronald J. Hy (Westport, Conn.: Greenwood Press).
Beverly A. Cigler (1988) "Current Policy Issues in Mitigation," pp. 39-52 in *Managing Disaster: Strategies and Policy Perspectives*, edited by Louise K. Comfort (Durham, NC: Duke University Press).
Bruce B. Clary (1985) "The Evolution and Structure of Natural Hazards Policies," *Public Administration Review* 45 (January): 20-28.
Congressional Research Service, Library of Congress (1984) Information Technology for Emergency Management, Report for the Subcommittee on Investigations and Oversight, Committee on Science and Technology, U.S. House of Representatives, 98th Congress, 2nd Session, October 9 (Washington, DC: U.S. Goverment Printing Office).
Thomas E. Drabek (1987) *The Professional Emergency Manager* (Boulder, Colo.: Program on Environment and Behavior, Institute of Behavioral Science, University of Colorado, Monograph #44).
Federal Emergency Management Agency (1983) *Process Overview: Integrated Emergency Management System* (Washington, DC: FEMA, CPG 1-100, September).
Ronald J. Hy and William L. Waugh, Jr. (1990) "The Emergency Management Function," in *Emergency Management Handbook*, edited by William L. Waugh, Jr., and Ronald J. Hy (Westport, Conn.: Greenwood Press).
Josephine M. LaPlante (1988) "Recovery Following Disaster: Policy Issues and Dimensions," pp. 217-235 in *Managing Disaster: Strategies and Policy Perspectives*, edited by Louise K. Comfort (Durham, NC: Duke University Press).
Ralph G. Lewis (1988) "Management Issues in Emergency Response,"

pp. 163-179 in *Managing Disaster: Strategies and Policy Perspectives*, edited by Louise K. Comfort (Durham, NC: Duke University Press).

David McLoughlin (1985) "A Framework for Integrated Emergency Management," *Public Administration Review* 45 (January): 165-172.

Peter J. May (1985) "FEMA's Role in Emergency Management: Recent Experience," *Public Administration Review* 45 (January): 40-48.

Peter J. May and Walter Williams (1986) *Disaster Policy Implementation: Managing Programs Under Shared Governance* (New York and London: Plenum Press).

Peter J. May (1988) "Disaster Recovery and Reconstruction," pp. 236-251 in *Managing Disaster: Strategies and Policy Perspectives*, edited by Louise K. Comfort (Durham, NC: Duke University Press).

National Governors' Association (1979) *Comprehensive Emergency Management: A Governor's Guide* (Washington, DC: U.S. Government Printing Office).

Ronald W. Perry (1985) *Comprehensive Emergency Management: Evacuating Threatened Populations* (Greenwich, Conn., and London: JAI Press).

William J. Petak (1985) "Emergency Management: A Challenge for Public Administration," *Public Administration Review* 45 (January): 3-7.

Linda Richter and William L. Waugh, Jr. (1986) "Terrorism and Tourism as Logical Companions," *Tourism Management* (January): 230-238.

U.S. General Accounting Office (1980a) *States Can Be Better Prepared to Respond to Disasters*, Washington, DC: U.S.G.A.O., CED-80-60, March 31.

U.S. General Accounting Office (1980b) *Three Mile Island: The Most Studied Nuclear Accident in History*, Washington, DC: U.S.G.A.O., EMD-80-109, September 9.

U.S. General Accounting Office (1983a) *Review of the Federal Emergency Management Agency's Role in Assisting State and Local Governments to Develop Hurricane Preparedness Planning*, Washington, DC: U.S.G.A.O., GAO/RCED-83-182, July 7.

U.S. General Accounting Office (1983b) *Stronger Direction Needed for the National Earthquake Program*, Washington, DC: U.S.G.A.O., GAO/RCED-83-103, July 26.

U.S. General Accounting Office (1983c) *Consolidation of Federal Assistance Resources Will Enhance the Federal-State Emergency Management Effort*, Washington, DC: U.S.G.A.O., GAO/GGD-83-92, August 30.

U.S. General Accounting Office (1984a) *The Federal Emergency Manage-*

ment Agency's Plan for Revitalizing U.S. Civil Defense: A Review of Three Major Plan Components, Washington, DC: U.S.G.A.O., GAO/ NSIAD-84-11, April 16.

U.S. General Accounting Office (1984b) *Further Actions Needed to Improve Emergency Preparedness Around Nuclear Plants*, Washington, DC: U.S.G.A.O., GAO/RCED-84-43, August 1.

William L. Waugh, Jr. (1988) "Policy and Implementation Issues in Disaster Preparedness," pp. 111-25 in *Managing Disasters: Strategies and Policy Perspectives*, edited by Louise K. Comfort (Durham, NC: Duke University Press)

William L. Waugh, Jr. (1989) "Emergency Management and the Capacities of State and Local Governments," in *Cities and Disaster: North American Studies in Emergency Management*, edited by Richard T. Sylves and William L. Waugh, Jr. (Springfield, Ill.: Charles C. Thomas Publishers).

William L. Waugh, Jr. (1990) "Volcanic Hazards," in *Emergency Management Handbook*, edited by William L. Waugh, Jr., and Ronald J. Hy (Westport, Conn.: Greenwood Press).

Chapter 3

THE TERRORISM PROCESS AND ANTITERRORISM POLICY

INTRODUCTION

While terrorist violence poses a risk for nearly everyone in the world, albeit generally without high probability, the phenomenon continues to confound policymakers' abilities to respond effectively. Despite the low probability of becoming involved in a terrorist act, the potential for large-scale destruction and mass casualties strongly suggests that action should be taken to reduce the vulnerability of society to the violence. In other words, the management of the risk of terrorism, the violent events, and the resultant effects are of paramount importance. To date, fortunately, the violence has largely been relatively focused and of low intensity. There have been few cases outside of war that have resulted in mass destruction and mass casualties. Notwithstanding that good fortune, the potential for large-scale destruction requires that we consider the consequences and develop strategies to prepare for, mitigate the effects of, respond to, and recover from such events.

The need to prepare for the possibility of large-scale terrorist violence is manifest. Communication, transportation, and energy networks are delicately structured. Water treatment, energy generation, and communication and transportation facilities tend to be very centralized. Population centers concentrate civilians and government officials. In short, major disruptions could result from relatively simple acts of violence, if strategically conducted. Sophisticated weapons and technologies are available, as well. Catastrophic terrorist events are well within the realm of possibility. The vulnerability of modern societies, the technologies of war, and the political motivations of incumbent elites and their challengers make terrorism an attractive tactic for the strong and the weak. Whether born of ideology or anger or economic interest, terrorism can focus violence and maximize its effect.

THE NATURE OF TERRORIST VIOLENCE

There are few political phenomena which evoke as much dread as terrorism. The violence associated with terrorism evokes a strong, negative response. At the same time, there are few phenomena which are as greatly misunderstood. That negative connotation and the confusion caused by the multiplicity of acts that might be characterized as "terroristic" have confounded the pursuit of a clear, unequivocal definition for the study of the phenomenon, as well as a consensually based legal definition to facilitate concerted international action to discourage the use of the tactic. Truly it is a case of where you stand on the issue depends on where you sit (Waugh, 1982 and 1986). Perspective is all important.

The origin of the phenomenon of terrorism is unclear. Some analysts trace the beginning of terrorist violence to the very beginning of intra- and intercommunal conflict, to our cave-dwelling ancestors. Modern terroristic violence, however, has generally been characterized as a post–World War II development, albeit occasionally traced to the terror implicit in the German bombing of London, the Allied bombings of Dresden and other cities, and the U.S. bombings of Hiroshima and Nagasaki. The military origins of contemporary terrorism may also be discerned from the increasing fuzziness between combatants and noncombatants. Civilian populations are targets in both terrorism and nuclear warfare.

Interest in political terrorism grew with the national liberation struggles of the postwar era in Indochina, Palestine, Cyprus, Algeria, the Congo, and elsewhere (Gross, 1958: Barker, 1959; Crozier, 1960; Arendt, 1963; Fanon, 1963; Carr, 1964; Brinton, 1965; Hutchison, 1978). Virtually all sides in all the conflicts of that era used terroristic tactics. The violence, however, was largely confined to the traditionally recognized combatants with few civilian casualties. More recently, terrorism has assumed other forms and, as a result, has been defined in a variety of ways. A look at the major perspectives or models may be instructive.

By and large, there are six principal models of terrorism:

1. The revolution or national liberation model,
2. The civil disorder model,
3. The law enforcement model,
4. The international conflict or surrogate warfare model,
5. The human rights or repressive violence model, and,
6. The vigilante model.

The models are frequently misapplied and almost always misunderstood. The thesis being addressed here is the problem inherent in applying assumptions about terrorism that will not hold true in a particular case, i.e., the problem of generalization. The models represent basic assumptions about terroristic events. In terms of effective policymaking, the models are critical variables in how terrorism is viewed by policymakers and the public and how policies and programs are designed to respond to terrorist violence. The interpretation of the violence, for example, often determines the agencies having jurisdiction or responsibility in the preparedness, mitigation, response, and recovery functions of emergency management. Military responses, one would assume, are not appropriate for largely civilian law enforcement problems. The military and police functions are quite different.

In general terms the six models represent the perspectives of most antiterrorism policymakers, but not all perspectives on the phenomenon. The revolution model developed out of the national liberation war experience and reflects the assumption of military, as well as political, objectives and the expectation of escalation if the violence is not checked. The civil disorder model developed out of the political turmoil of the 1960s, particularly in the industrialized democracies, and reflects the notion that terrorism is simply an extreme form of dissent, while the law enforcement model is essentially the corollary to that view based on the police perspective on the challenge to government authority recognizing the challenge but not the political nature of the acts (see Allen, 1974).

The international conflict model represents a dominant view in policymaking and has colored U.S. antiterrorism efforts in that it links most terroristic violence to the U.S.-Soviet conflict. Virtually all terrorist acts, by this Cold War model, are interpreted as gains or losses for the superpowers. Terrorist organizations are assumed to be controlled by or allied to one side or the other. There are slight variations on the theme depending upon whether the terrorists are perceived to be acting as surrogates for a superpower or largely acting alone but in the interests of the superpower. Cuba, for example, would be perceived as a surrogate if supporting terrorism but Iran or Libya would confuse the issue somewhat. Failure to ratify antiterrorism agreements is construed as providing support to the other side. The human rights or repressive violence model has generally been applied to violence used by incumbent elites, usually government authorities or their agents, against their own citizens. And, finally, the vigilante model has been recognized more in recent years with the increased amount of right-wing violence in the U.S. and Western Europe. The repressive violence model is perhaps the oldest view of terrorism, but it has only recently become an influential perspective among policymakers in the U.S. A brief look at each of those models will demonstrate how they affect policymaking.

Revolutionary Terrorism

For many analysts and scholars terrorism is a revolutionary strategy or tactic characterized by low-level violence against symbolic representatives of a government or political elite, with few direct attacks on the police and military forces enforcing the policies and protecting the officials of that regime. The model is generally based on the national liberation experience of the 1940s and 1950s. Terrorism defined by this revolution model is low-intensity violence that may or may not lead to high-intensity campaigns directed against the very foundations of the regime.

The model is implicit in much of the literature focusing on the military response to terrorism (Greene, 1962; Galula, 1964; Paget, 1967; Kitson, 1971; Clutterbuck, 1973, 1975, 1977; Mallin, 1977), but it is not restricted to military analysts. Terrorism is viewed as the low end of the continuum of violence leading to guerrilla warfare and ultimately civil war (Hutchinson, 1972). Military responses to terrorism usually are based on the assumptions that terrorist organizations: (1) will choose military targets or victims if they have the capacity to attack such targets; (2) have the potential to escalate their violence; and, (3) have broad, "revolutionary" political objectives. Revolutionary terrorists have the goal of overthrowing the incumbent elite, if not the entire regime, and, thus, cannot be negotiated with seriously without jeopardizing the legitimacy of the regime and/or compromising its authority. Studies of terrorist strategies and objectives, however, indicate that the objectives may be quite limited and may, in fact, be based upon legitimate grievances against the government or other economic elites (see, for example: Wilkinson, 1974; Crenshaw, 1981; Waugh, 1983).

Civil Disorder Model

The civil disorder model was a product of the study of domestic political strife during the 1960s and early 1970s, as well as perhaps influenced by the existential literature of the period and the

politics of the New Left. By this model, terrorism is viewed as a
product of deep-seated frustration among the alienated and/or
repressed (whether that frustration is viewed as being legitimate
or not). The model provides a sympathetic view of terroristic
action, although not necessary an apology or a vindication, for
analysts examining the socioeconomic precipitants of the violence.

During the 1970s, scholars searched out the variables that
would explain the elevation of political conflict from economic
and election boycotts, to demonstrations and strikes to the use of
violent confrontation (Davies, 1962, 1971; Thornton, 1964; Eckstein, 1965; Gurr, 1971; Feierabend, Feierabend, and Gurr, 1972).
While inconclusive, the theories did offer some explanation and
suggested some policy responses. Terrorism was an under-
standable extension of protest in the "revolution of rising
expectations." Models of economic development and "transitional societies" provided some explanation for the violent
phenomena as a response to confused or disintegrating social and
political institutions or simply the speed of change. Stability in
terms of reduced violence, according to the theorists, could be
achieved by slowing the disintegration of traditional institutions
and encouraging the development of new ones. More recently a
few commentators have suggested that authoritarian governments may serve to stabilize transitional societies by providing
both stable institutions and decisive allocations of scarce resources. Notwithstanding those debates, the assumptions inherent in
this model suggest that policymakers focus on the precipitants of
the violence to assure that it does not escalate.

In psychological terms, this model has also been associated
with "angry violence" or violence intended to inflict pain or
injury, rather than instrumental violence (Davies, 1977: 10-11).
Some of the very short-lived organizations in the U.S. during the
1960s turbulent racial and anti-war clashes might well be
characterized as practitioners of angry violence rather than
"terrorists." The nihilist organizations involved in terrorist campaigns, mostly in Japan and Western Europe, during the 1970s

may fit this pattern, as well. Removing the precipitants of the anger, it is thought, will effectively eliminate the violent behavior.

Law Enforcement Model

Another common interpretation can be found in the law enforcement model in which the political objectives of the terrorists are considered mutations of the economic objectives sought by criminals who use essentially the same tactics. Blackmail, kidnapping, extortion, bank robbery, burglary, and other illegal acts by political terrorists are viewed in much the same way as any other criminal acts. The differences, as noted by law enforcement officials, are found in the levels of commitment, the fanaticism, of political terrorists which affect hostage negotiation processes, the choices of targets, and the potential for escalation if political and/or economic support is found by the group. The political motivations are not seen as mitigating factors in the police response. The focus is simply on the violation of law, rather than on the broader concerns raised by the causes of the violence.

By this model, the options of policymakers are few. Negotiation with criminals is not usually considered an option, except to the extent that it may be a useful tactic to gain advantage over them. Political objectives are not recognized or, generally, negotiated because that would lend some legitimacy to the terrorists.

International Conflict Model(s)

Other analysts and scholars view terrorism as an extension of traditional, albeit not necessarily lawful or accepted, modes of international conflict (Fromkin, 1975). Terrorist tactics have been common among national strategies of war, from the rocket attacks and bombing of London by the Luftwaffe to the bombing of Hiroshima during World War II. Today's terrorism, by the view, may be a logical tactic of nations desiring to avoid more open political or military conflict or lacking the resources to sustain the more conventional forms of military conflict. As a military tactic, terrorism permits the projection of national power against nations or people that are distant with little expense in personnel and materials and, if clandestine, with little danger of major political costs. A terrorist force can inflict considerable economic damage on an enemy nation as well as eliminate hostile leaders (Richter and Waugh, 1986). The international conflict model is significant in a number of respects, not least of which is the notion that individuals are not units of analysis and are not considered major actors in the events in which they participated willingly or unwillingly. Terrorism and its threat is interpreted almost wholly in terms of national interests and honor. In that context, negotiation is difficult unless both sides can appear to win.

The surrogate warfare and proxy warfare concepts in international relations are based on the international conflict model. Terrorist activity is simply an extension of existing international animosities and terrorist organizations are controlled, or at least strongly influenced, by one side or the other. The existence of independent states outside of the two superpower camps is not generally recognized. The "one man's terrorist is another man's freedom fighter" cliché is particularly apt with this model.

Human Rights or Repressive Violence Model

Increasingly analysts and scholars are examining terrorism as a tactic of incumbent elites to protect their political privilege and wealth. There is a thin line between a regime's use of police and military forces to maintain civic order and political stability and its use of such force to repress political opposition. The human rights model focuses on those uses of power that are fundamental to nations and on the illegitimate use of that power. Terrorism defined in these normative terms, whether be it violence sponsored by official representatives of the regime or by terrorist groups tolerated or sanctioned by the regime, takes on a different cast (Stohl and Lopez, 1984; Stohl, Carleton, Lopez, and Samuels,

1986; Stohl and Lopez, 1987; Stohl, Carleton, and Lopez, 1988). The concept of repressive terrorism generally assumes that the public(or known) manifestations of the violence are only the most overt and gross forms and that the violence can escalate and intensify if unchecked.

The first policy problem is to determine the scope of the violence. That is an extremely difficult task when the government is uncooperative and there are few other agencies willing to risk becoming involved. The second problem, assuming that the repression is not part of a larger regime policy, is that of dealing with governmental institutions, such as the military and police, that resist attempts at reform.

The Vigilante Model

Vigilante terrorism is a variation of the repressive form mentioned above. The distinction, however, is that vigilantism is not normally supported by the regime, although the objectives of the vigilantes may be to preserve the very values promoted by the regime and which may be crucial to its continued existence. The use of violence by groups supporting regime policies or societal norms is also not a new phenomenon. Such groups may supplant the authority of the state by replacing its enforcement agencies.

Other interpretations can be rooted in the legal, psychological, or other concerns of the analyst or commentator, but, by and large, they are based on one of the six models above. Thus far, even the analyses of terrorist activity within regions (Halperin, 1976; Lodge, 1981; Alexander and Myers, 1982) have not identified geographic variables that might explain all types of terrorism.

In policy terms, the determination of the most applicable model can have a profound impact on the design of antiterrorism policies and programs. The literature on terrorism is full of injunctions to avoid overreacting to terrorist violence, particularly when the response threatens the civil liberties and civil rights of the citizenry (Wilkinson, 1977; Bell, 1978).

Definitions of Terrorism

Despite the confusion caused by the variety of perspectives on terrorist violence, there are common elements in the definitions of terrorism currently being used by scholars, analysts, and policy-makers. In general terms, the definitions usually include four elements:

1. Terrorism involves the use or threat of extraordinary violence,
2. Terrorism is goal-directed (or rational) behavior;
3. Terrorism is intended to have a psychological impact beyond the immediate victims, and
4. Terrorists choose their victims largely for their symbolic, rather than their instrumental, value (Waugh, 1982: 27).

In short, terrorism is the use or credible threat of violence that is out of the ordinary, for political objectives, with an intended impact broader than the immediate victims (human or otherwise) who were chosen for their symbolic value.

The threat of violence may be latent to the extent that the targets view it as real even though there is no overt attempt by the terrorist organization or regime to make the threat more obvious. "Latent terrorism" is characteristic of regimes that have used extraordinary violence to repress dissent in the past and no longer have to express threats to intimidate potential dissenters (Dallin and Breslauer, 1970). "Latent terrorism" may also result when other groups have established reputations for dealing harshly with opponents, although non-state terrorists may have to reaffirm their reputations for violence more frequently.

That terrorism involves extraordinary violence suggests that the kinds of "latent terrorism" found in some regimes may not fit the usual definition of terrorism. No state has explicitly condoned the use of terroristic violence against its own citizens, although the legally sanctioned police and regulatory powers of a state may be quite broad, so most applications can be characterized as extra-ordinary.

Terrorism is goal-directed, hence rational, behavior. Intent is crucial to the definition of terrorism which suggests a conscious and premeditated application of violence to achieve a state of terror. The choice of victims for their symbolic value further affirms the rationality of the tactic. The necessary distinction is between victims and targets. Political terrorism is a form of political communication that involves the use or threat of violence to influence the behavior of a target group, usually government officials, for political ends. The communication is of two kinds: the threat of violence and the political message (Alexander, 1976). When victims are killed, they are not terrorized. Their deaths are intended to send a political message to the real target group.

The choice of victims for their symbolic, rather than their in-strumental, value recognizes that terrorism is seldom the tactic of strong political groups. In fact, most conceptualizations suggest that terrorism is always practiced by groups, never individuals, and that it is low-intensity violence. The revolution model is based on the view that terrorism is always low-level violence and that when the level of violence increases and the targets become in-strumental, i.e., police and military personnel, the violence can more properly be termed guerrilla warfare or civil war. Weak political groups can seldom muster the necessary resources to direct their attacks against the very pillars supporting the authority of the regime. That is not to say, however, that instrumental targets are never chosen. By this definition, the warfare in Belfast may be more properly termed guerrilla warfare or civil war, rather than terrorism. The nature of the attacks on Ulster police and British military personnel would bear out that conclusion. Much the same can be said of the Palestinian conflict with Israel. In both cases, the level of "terror" has reached an intensity at which residents appear numb, no longer any more intimidated by the violent acts. Indeed, in Beirut and Belfast, one can find persons appearing to attend to their daily routines oblivious to the gunfire and explosions.

THE PROCESS OF TERRORISM

For purposes of simplification and explication, the process of terrorism can be modelled. Figures 1 to 6 illustrate the process of terrorism as it may be viewed in the six models. By and large the process is similar in each case. There are three primary actors or sets of actors:

1. The terrorists,
2. The victims, be they people, buildings or other inanimate objects, and
3. The targets of the violence, those the terrorists are seeking to influence.

There are also three secondary actors or sets of actors:

1. The nontargeted or spectator domestic audience,
2. The nontargeted or spectator international audience, and
3. The government or governments responsible for responding to the violence.

The responsible governments may be several, based on territorial jurisdiction over the events; nationality of the victims; legal jurisdiction based on something other than territory; or involvement in the event as a target, terrorist, or victim.

The process of terrorism itself has six elements:

1. The use or threat of violence,
2. The violent message to the target group,
3. The political message or action sought from the target group,
4. The broader communication of the threat and political message to domestic and international audiences and to responsible governments,
5. The reaction of the target group to the threat and the

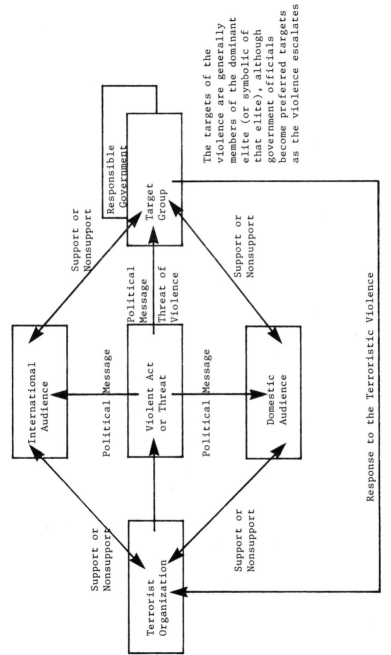

FIGURE 1 Revolutionary terrorism.

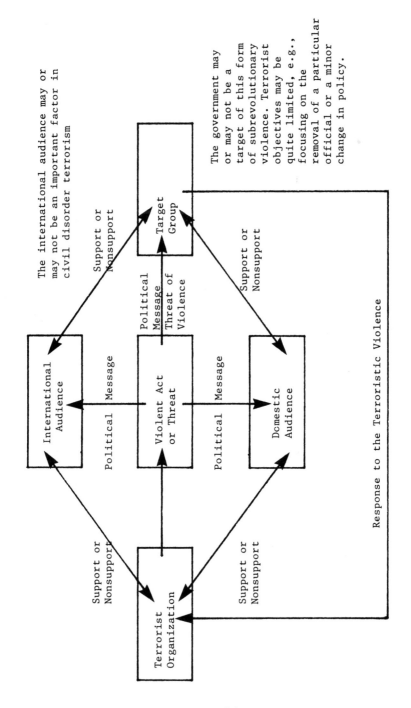

The international audience may or may not be an important factor in civil disorder terrorism

The government may or may not be a target of this form of subrevolutionary violence. Terrorist objectives may be quite limited, e.g., focusing on the removal of a particular official or a minor change in policy.

FIGURE 2 Civil disorder terrorism.

54

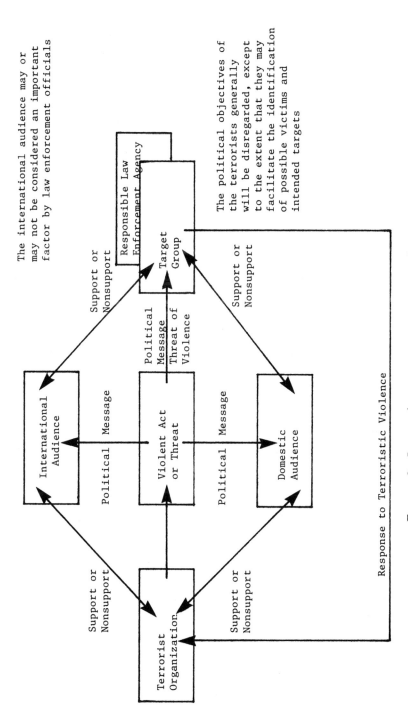

The international audience may or may not be considered an important factor by law enforcement officials

The political objectives of the terrorists generally will be disregarded, except to the extent that they may facilitate the identification of possible victims and intended targets

Responsible Law Enforcement Agency

Target Group

Support or Nonsupport

Political Message Threat of Violence

Support or Nonsupport

International Audience

Political Message

Violent Act or Threat

Political Message

Domestic Audience

Support or Nonsupport

Support or Nonsupport

Terrorist Organization

Response to Terroristic Violence

FIGURE 3   Law enforcement perspective on domestic terrorism.

55

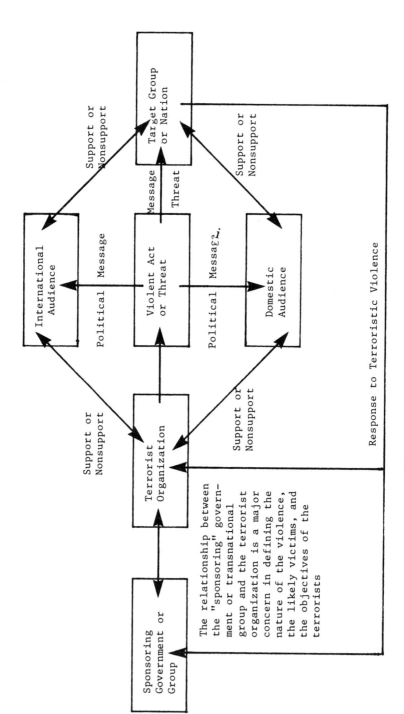

FIGURE 4 International conflict terrorism.

Target Group or Nation

Support or Nonsupport

Message

Threat

Support or Nonsupport

International Audience

Political Message

Violent Act or Threat

Political Message

Domestic Audience

Support or Nonsupport

Terrorist Organization

Support or Nonsupport

Response to Terroristic Violence

Sponsoring Government or Group

The relationship between the "sponsoring" government or transnational group and the terrorist organization is a major concern in defining the nature of the violence, the likely victims, and the objectives of the terrorists

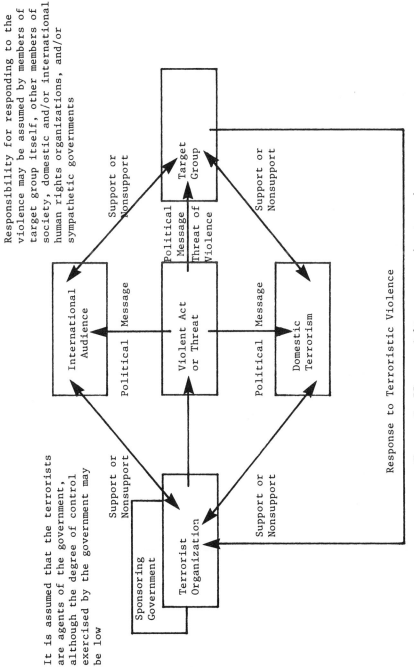

It is assumed that the terrorists are agents of the government, although the degree of control exercised by the government may be low

Responsibility for responding to the violence may be assumed by members of target group itself, other members of society, domestic and/or international human rights organizations, and/or sympathetic governments

FIGURE 5   Human rights or repression terrorism.

57

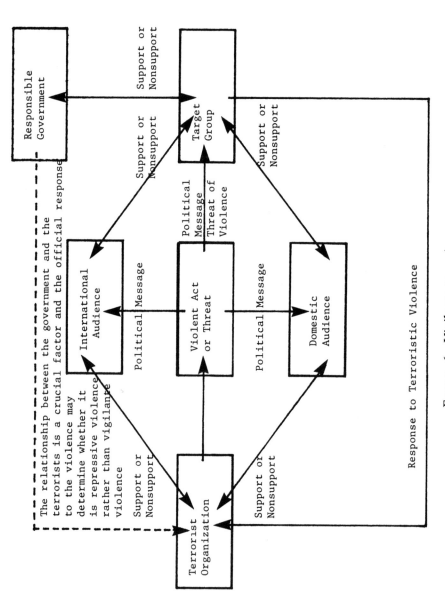

The relationship between the government and the terrorists is a crucial factor and the official response to the violence may determine whether it is repressive violence rather than vigilante violence

FIGURE 6 Vigilante terrorism.

political message (e.g., compliance with the terrorists' demands, change in policy, or change in personnel);
6. The responses of all the audiences to the political conflict between the terrorists and the targets (e.g., expressions of support for one side or the other, apathy, or interventions in the conflict).

THEORIES OF RESPONSE

Prescriptions to deal with terrorist violence can generally be categorized as suggesting that governments or other agencies:

1. Eliminate the causes of the violence,
2. Increase the costs of using terrorism, or
3. Deny terrorists the benefits they seek.

The elimination of the precipitants of terrorist violence, as a policy, is not a frequently mentioned alternative. The earlier discussion of "angry violence" suggested that the removal of the causes of the frustration-aggression reactions may eliminate the desire to inflict pain or injury. For the small number of terrorists who may be motivated by anger rather than more instrumental objectives, that response may be most appropriate. One cannot overlook the possibility that the political objectives of terrorists may be commendable and not antithetical to the existing political order. The political issues should not be confused with the moral issues raised by the choice of terrorism. In the long run, a regime may find it much less expensive to redress legitimate grievances. Some terrorists, moreover, may seek very narrow, limited objectives that can rather easily be addressed, i.e., "subrevolutionary" terrorists (Wilkinson, 1974). The problems for policymakers may be in separating the redress of grievances from the violence to avoid the appearance that terrorism is an effective tool. If the violent tactic is chosen because there are no other realistic means of effecting change, the provision of forum for the expression of grievances would be suggested.

Increasing the costs of using terrorism is a frequent prescription given by analysts. The attention to security and punishment policy options is attributable to the prominence of the law enforcement and military models of terrorism. The first objective is to deny terrorists the opportunity to commit acts of violence against the targets that they would prefer. It is impossible to protect all possible targets from terrorist violence, but some targets may be secured. The second objective is to increase the costs of committing acts of terrorism by forcing terrorists to expend scarce resources (financial, material, and human) on more dangerous acts of violence. Increased security can increase that danger as can actions that make it difficult to use the less expensive forms of violence, such as bombs. Security can also include denying terrorists some of the resources necessary to carry out their violence, such as strictly regulating access to guns, particularly automatic weapons and handguns, and making it difficult for suspected terrorists to travel freely.

International conventions can provide other means of securing possible targets and assuring the apprehension and punishment of known terrorists. The third objective in increasing the costs of using terrorism is the assurrance of punishment. Effective law enforcement can speed the attrition of scarce human resources in terrorist organizations. Punishment is a particular problem when the violence is international because of the lack of a strong international consensus against terrorism, differences in how the violence is perceived, and the scarcity of effective mechanisms to support multilateral action against terrorists. Extradition treaties are generally bilateral. Many northern European and South American nations have very strong traditions of granting political asylum, which may conflict with requests for extradition when the guilt of a "terrorist" is uncertain. The principle of *aut punire aut dedere,*suggesting that all nations should try terrorists or extradite them to a nation that will, is not consistent with other political values, in other words.

The likelihood of strong, concerted international action to

assure the punishment of terrorists is not promising given the differences in how terrorism may be defined. Much more success has been realized when there has been general agreement on the definition or on the outlawing of a particular tactic, such as attacks on aircraft and on diplomatic personnel and facilities.

The third option, denial of the benefits of terrorism, finds wide support in the literature. It is the basis of the U.S. and Israeli policies of "no negotiation, no compromise," although indications are that compromises are made, particularly in the U.S., when the acts of violence and the benefits are separated *or* when the compromise can be done without publicity.

Denial of benefits is perhaps most often associated with responses to international terrorism. That may in large measure be due to the level of analysis in international affairs (Lopez, 1982). As mentioned in the discussion of the international conflict model of terrorism, when states are confronted with violence which may be sponsored by another state there is less inclination to consider the human costs involved in the negotiations.

Denial of benefits also presupposes that the objectives of the terrorist organization can be identified. Denial of the tactical objectives, usually money, prisoner releases, publicity, and/or safe passage/asylum, can reduce the ability of the organization to operate. Denial of the strategic objectives (publicity, punishment, organizational imperatives, provocation, disruption, and/or instrumental gains) can reduce the effectiveness of the organization. And, denial of the ideological or ultimate objectives of the terrorists may be essential to the preservation of the current regime or order (see Waugh, 1982, 1983).

The theories of response are more complex than suggested here, and there are many more policy options associated with each. But, the brief descriptions should provide some background for understanding how governments and other agencies can intervene in the process of terrorism to eliminate the causes of the violence, increase the costs of using terrorism, and deny terrorists the benefits they seek. As will be suggested, several approaches may be necessary to provide an effective response to terrorism.

INTERVENING IN THE PROCESS OF TERRORISM

The six models of terrorism offer a variety of alternative policy options to intervene in the process and alter the effect sought by the terrorists. To simplify the identification of policy interventions, the revolutionary model and the repressive violence model are used in Figures 7 and 8 to indicate the principal opportunities for disrupting the terrorism process.

The intervention models suggest that the process of terrorism can be interrupted and, perhaps, disrupted by effective antiterrorism policies. The basic assumption is that a government or another agency has determined that a problem exists and is acting to arrest the violence. That certainly is not always the case, as the government itself or one of its agencies may be the terrorist organization, government officials may be tacitly or more overtly supporting the terrorists, or the government may simply not be capable of containing or eliminating the violence.

Figure 7 generally represents the revolution, civil disorder, law enforcement, and vigilante models. It assumes that the government will respond to reduce or eliminate the terroristic violence, although there may be some differences in how a government might respond to each kind of violence. Nonetheless, the figure does indicate in general terms how a government might respond to terrorism.

To intervene in the process of terrorism, a government might:

1. Prepare for possible violence in terms of preparing contingency plans, developing intelligence gathering capabilities, creating special antiterrorism forces, designating lead agencies and allocating resources to support antiterrorism institutions, and determining the level of threat that might be posed by a terrorist campaign or event;

2. Mold the environment to make it less conducive to and supportive of terrorist violence in terms of increasing public awareness of the phenomenon and encouraging public support of the government's policies, building legislative and popular mandates for preferred government responses, encouraging bi-

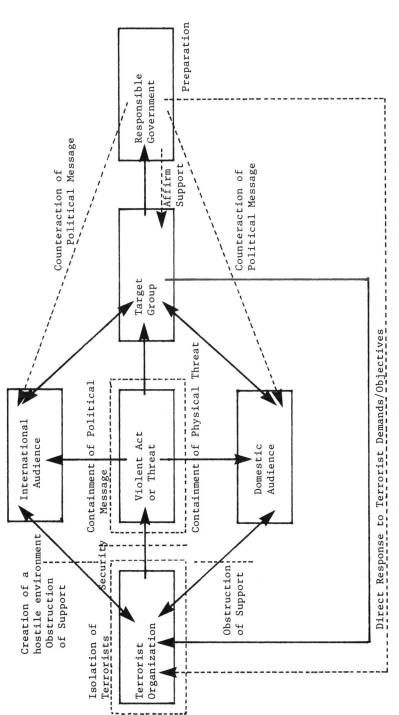

FIGURE 7   Policy interventions in nonstate-sponsored terrorism.

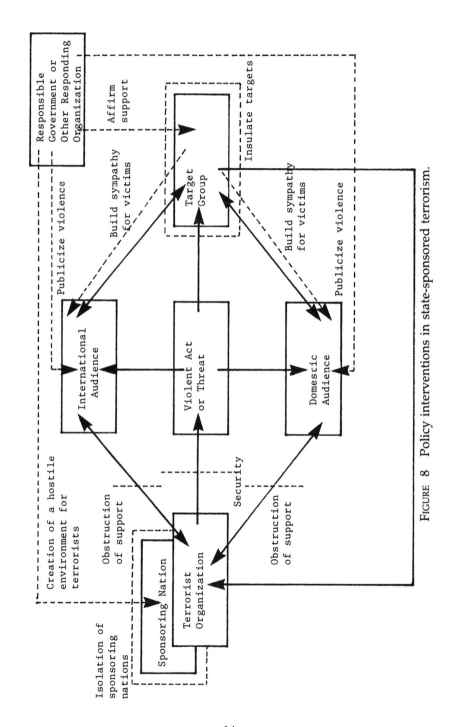

FIGURE 8 Policy interventions in state-sponsored terrorism.

64

lateral and multilateral agreements consistent with the government's perspective on the violence, and creating a climate of intolerance toward terroristic violence;

3. Alleviate the conditions that are either precipitating the violent actions or provide alternative means for opposition groups to express their dissent;

4. Deny the terrorists the opportunity to use violence by providing security for all likely victims (human or otherwise), at least to the extent feasible;

5. Contain the physical destruction caused by the terrorists by quickly removing debris, treating casualties, and restoring normal operations in the affected area to reduce the impact of the violence;

6. Contain the political message implicit in the violence by limiting and structuring the publication or broadcast of terrorist statements;

7. Counteract the communication of terrorist propaganda by providing counterpropaganda, revealing the terrorists real, or broader motives, or focusing attention on the destruction (particularly loss of lives) to divert attention from the political goals of the terrorists;

8. Make the operational environment of the terrorists very inhospitable in terms of eliminating "safe houses," increasing surveillance of public areas to discover known and suspected terrorists, increasing police pressure on potential supporters, making it more difficult to secure arms and other essential materials, and so on;

9. Isolate the terrorists from domestic and international support by making it difficult to transport arms, monies, and other essential supplies across the border; increasing the penalties for supporting terrorist activities; making it more difficult for known or suspected terrorists to move from one state to another; and,

10. Respond to specific terrorist demands for ransom, releases of prisoners, publication or broadcast of political messages, political asylum or safe passage to another state, or other action.

Governments might choose one, several, or all of the above actions in response to terrorist violence and some may not be appropriate in particular circumstances. Other options are also possible. The general categories, however, do illustrate the variety of responses a government may have in a given situation. Resolution of an event, nonetheless, may not be possible in all cases.

Figure 8 illustrates the policy options available when terroristic violence is used by a state against its own citizens or other residents or against another state or another foreign target. The responding agent in this case would necessarily be another government, an international or transnational organization, or even a very influential domestic organization. Unfortunately, as the Carter administration found when it attempted to use compliance with the basic tenets of human rights as a criterion for determining eligibility for U.S. foreign aid and for recognizing a community of interest in values judged important to the U.S., such violence is difficult to measure in an objective sense and to address in a political sense. Certainly it is extremely difficult to protect people from their own government in terms of providing security, i.e., denying the government the opportunity to use violence, but it is possible to deny, at least in part, the terroristic government the benefits of its actions and to increase the costs of using the violence. "Repressive terrorism" is not considered a legitimate exercise of power in any state, although the vagueness of the term might permit some repressive policies to be supported by law and/or condoned in practice. All governments have the potential for repression by virtue of their regulatory and enforcement functions. Notwithstanding that ambiguity in the term and in the definition of fundamental human rights, there is a reasonable consensus on what political and social rights should be and what should not be permitted.

The response to the kinds of terrorism practiced by states or their agents against other states or foreign targets is also problematic. The clandestine support of terrorist violence by a government is difficult to prove and more difficult to stop. The current political climate, however, is such that governments may prefer not to be associated with terroristic violence, particularly of certain forms of terrorism such as aerial hijackings or attacks on diplomatic personnel and facilities. International public opinion can have a significant impact on a nation's economic development and, by extension, on its internal politics. In both cases of state-sponsored terrorism, the state may attempt to focus the violence on the target group, to contain its effects to minimize the communication of the political message and the threat to other domestic and international audiences. To counter such terrorism, the task then is to ensure that the communication is not effectively contained.

As Figure 8 indicates, to intervene in the process of state-sponsored terrorism an agency might:

1. Prepare for possible violence in terms of preparing contingency plans, developing intelligence gathering capabilities, creating special reaction forces, and designating lead agencies and allocating resources to support anti-terrorism institutions;

2. Mold the environment to make it less conducive to and supportive of state terrorism in terms of increasing public awareness of the phenomenon and encouraging public support for human rights principles, building legislative and popular mandates for human rights laws, encouraging international accords supportive of human rights, and creating a climate of intolerance toward state terrorism;

3. Encourage policy changes that will reduce the likelihood of official violence and provide other means of conflict resolution;

4. Deny the government (or its agents) the opportunity to use violence clandestinely by monitoring likely targets and obstructing terroristic acts to the extent possible;

5. Make it difficult for a terroristic state to contain or hide its violence;

6. Identifying and publicizing the political intent of the terrorist government and weighing that intent against the social costs;

7. Make the operational environment of the terrorists very inhospitable in terms of identifying and publicizing the names of the terrorists, seeking political and economic sanctions against the known terrorists, increasing popular pressure on the terrorists, and encouraging other states to deny the terrorist government materials and expertise that might be used in the application of repressive violence; and

8. Isolate the terrorists from domestic and international support by making it difficult to carry on normal economic and political activities.

Here, too, agencies might choose one, several, or all of the above actions in response to terrorist violence and some may not be feasible or appropriate in certain circumstances. Undoubtedly, it is difficult to respond to state-sponsored terrorism because of the problems in gaining access to the locations where it is being practiced and political leverage sufficient to influence the behavior of the regime. Humanitarian appeals may be effective in some cases and not in others. The application of effective sanctions against such states is also problemmatic. Nonetheless, it is important to consider the phenomenon of terrorism in terms of its use by states as well as by non-state actors. As will be noted later, effective antiterrorism efforts may well depend upon the example provided by the regime itself. High levels of terrorist violence in France and Mexico in the 1970s and 1980s, for example, have been attributed to the tolerance shown those using political violence. Both nations extol the revolutionary values that shaped their histories, including in some measure the violence that characterized those revolutionary times.   In any case, managing state-sponsored terrorist events may prove to be more important than managing other terrorist events.

MANAGING TERRORIST EVENTS: THE CHALLENGE

Certainly it is no easy task to manage the risk of terrorism and respond to its occurrance. As the preceding discussion indicates, there are numerous opportunities to intervene in the process of terrorism, whether state-sponsored or not, or at least to prepare for such interventions. The discussions of the models of terrorism were intended to demonstrate that the perception of the problem, the threat or reality of terrorism, may be all important in designing effective emergency management efforts. Certainly the perspective will influence the policy options that are considered.

Terrorism presents a risk that must be weighed, just like other hazards or potential disasters. Analysts usually begin with assessments of risk, including the probability of a disaster and potential intensity. Probability increases when political conditions are supportive of the violence, when geographic location facilitates terrorist activity, when there is significant exposure in terms of likely terrorist targets, and when political and administrative mechanisms to deal with terrorism are ineffective.

The thesis here is that terrorism may present a significant danger to a particular society, and effective emergency management procedures can reduce that danger.

REFERENCES

Yonah Alexander, ed. (1976) *International Terrorism: National, Regional, and Global Perspectives* (New York: Praeger).

Francis A. Allen (1974) *The Crimes of Politics: Political Dimensions of Criminal Justice* (Cambridge, Mass.: Harvard University Press).

Hannah Arendt (1963) *On Revolution* (New York: Viking Press).

Dudley Barker (1959) *Grivas: Portrait of a Terrorist* (New York: Harcourt, Brace and Company).

J. Bowyer Bell (1971) *The Myth of the Guerrilla* (New York:Knopf)

J. Bowyer Bell (1973) "Contemporary Revolutionary Organizations," in *Transnational Relations and World Politics*, pp. 153-68, edited by Robert O. Keohane and Joseph S. Nye, Jr. (Cambridge, Mass.: Harvard University Press).

J. Bowyer Bell (1975) *Transnational Terror* (Washington, D.C.: American Enterprise Institute).

J. Bowyer Bell (1976) *On Revolt: Strategies of National Liberation* (Cambridge, Mass.: Harvard University Press).

J. Bowyer Bell (1978) *A Time of Terror: How Democratic Societies Respond to Revolutionary Violence* (New York: Basic Books)

Crane Brinton (1965) *The Anatomy of Revolution* (New York: Vintage Books).

E. H. Carr (1964) *Studies in Revolution* (New York: Grosset and Dunlap).

Richard Clutterbuck (1973) *Protest and the Urban Guerrilla* (London: Cassell).

Richard Clutterbuck (1975) *Living with Terrorism* (New Rochelle, N.Y.: Arlington House Publishers).

Richard Clutterbuck (1977) *Guerrillas and Terrorists* (London: Faber and Faber, Ltd.)

Martha Crenshaw (1981) "The Causes of Terrorism," *Comparative Politics* 13 (July): 379-399.

Brian Crozier (1960) *The Rebels: A Study of Postwar Insurrections* (Boston: Beacon Press).

Brian Crozier (1974) *Transnational Terrorism* (Gaithersburg, Md.: International Association of Chiefs of Police).

Alexander Dallin and George W. Breslauer (1970) *Political Terror in Communist Systems* (Stanford, Calif.: Stanford University Press).

James C. Davies (1962) "Toward a Theory of Revolution," *American Sociological Review* 27 (February): 5-19.

James C. Davies, ed. (1971) *When Men Rebel and Why* (New York: Free Press).

Thomas R. Davies (1977) "Feedback Processes and International Terrorism," Ph.D. Dissertation, Florida State University (Ann Arbor, Mich.: University Microfilms).

Harry Eckstein (1964) *Internal War* (New York: Free Press).

Harry Eckstein (1965) "On the Etiology of Internal War," *History and Theory* 4: 133-163.

Frantz Fanon (1963) *The Wretched of the Earth* (New York: Grove Press).

Ivo K. Feierabend, Rosalind L. Feierabend, and Ted Robert Gurr, eds. (1972) *Anger, Violence, and Politics* (Englewood Cliffs, N.J.: Prentice-Hall).

David Fromkin (1975) "The Strategy of Terrorism," *Foreign Affairs* (July): 683-698.

David Galula (1964) *Counterinsurgency Warfare* (New York: Praeger)

T. N. Greene, ed. (1962) *The Guerrilla—And How to Fight Him* (New York: Praeger).

Feliks Gross (1958) *The Seizure of Power in a Century of Revolutions* (New York: Philosophical Library).

Ted Robert Gurr (1971) *Why Men Rebel* (Princeton, N.J.: Princeton

University Press)

Ernst Halperin (1976) *Terrorism in Latin America* (Beverly Hills, Calif.: Sage Publications).

Martha Crenshaw Hutchinson (1972) "The Concept of Revolutionary Terrorism," *Journal of Conflict Resolution* 16 (September): 383-396.

Martha Crenshaw Hutchinson (1978) *Revolutionary Terrorism: The FLN in Algeria, 1954-1962* (Stanford, Calif.: Hoover Institution Press).

Frank Kitson (1971) *Low Intensity Operations: Subversion, Insurgency, Peacekeeping* (London: Faber and Faber).

Juliet Lodge, ed. (1981) *Terrorism: A Challenge to the State* (New York: St. Martin's Press).

George A. Lopez (1982) "Terrorism, Worldviews and Problems of Policy," paper presented at the Annual Meeting of the International Studies Association, Cincinnati, Ohio, March 24-27.

Jay Mallin (1977) "Terrorism as a Military Weapon," *Air University Review* (January-February).

Julian Paget (1967) *Counter-Insurgency Operations* (New York: Walker).

Linda Richter and William L. Waugh, Jr. (1986) "Terrorism and Tourism as Logical Companions," *Tourism Management* (December): 230-238.

Michael Stohl and George A. Lopez, eds. (1984) *The State as Terrorist* (Westport, Conn.: Greenwood Press).

Michael Stohl, David Carleton, George A. Lopez, and Stephen Samuels (1986) "State Violation of Human Rights: Issues and Problems of Measurement," *Human Rights Quarterly* 8 (November): 592-606.

Michael Stohl and George A. Lopez, eds. (1987) *Government Violence and Repression: An Agenda for Research* (Westport, Conn.: Greenwood Press).

Michael Stohl, David Carleton, and George A. Lopez, eds. (1988) *Testing Theories of State Violence and Repression* (Westport, Conn.: Greenwood Press).

Thomas P. Thornton (1964) "Terror as a Weapon of Political Agitation," in *Internal War,* pp. 71-99, edited by Harry Eckstein (New York: Free Press).

William L. Waugh, Jr. (1982) *International Terrorism: How Nations Respond to Terrorists* (Chapel Hill, N.C.: Documentary Publications).

William L. Waugh, Jr. (1983) "The Values in Violence: The Organizational and Political Objectives of Terrorist Groups," *Conflict Quarterly* (Summer): 1-19.

William L. Waugh, Jr. (1986) "Integrating the Policy Models of Terrorism and Emergency Management," *Policy Studies Review* (Fall): 286-300.

William L. Waugh, Jr., and Jane P. Sweeney, eds. (1990) *Antiterrorism Policies: An International Comparison* (London: Routledge, forthcoming).
Paul Wilkinson (1974) *Political Terrorism* (London: Macmillan Press Ltd.)
Paul Wilkinson (1977) *Terrorism and the Liberal State* (New York: Wiley).

Chapter 4

INTEGRATING THE POLICY MODELS

The application of the emergency management models, both the four-phase policy model and the Integrated Emergency Management Systems model, to terrorism-related hazards and disasters is somewhat complicated by the ambiguous nature of the phenomenon of terrorism. The identification of the hazard and the assessment of risk are dependent upon the perspective taken. Likewise, the perspective will determine the lead agencies involved in mitigating the effects of, preparing for, responding to, and recovering from the disasters that occur as a result of terrorism.

In general terms, the two policy intervention models (Figures 7 and 8 in Chapter 3) indicated that the process of terrorism can be affected through:

1. Obstruction or denial of opportunity to attack a target,
2. Alteration of the terrorists' operational environment so that it is less supportive of violent activities,
3. Alleviation of conditions that may increase the frustration

of opposition political groups or significant segments of the population and thus precipitate violence,

4. Containment of the physical destruction resulting from terrorist attacks,
5. Containment of the threat implicit in the violent acts;
6. Counteraction of the political message communicated by the terrorists,
7. Reduction of the terrorists' freedom of movement,
8. Isolation of the terrorists' from international and domestic support, and
9. Response to specific demands.

Both models also suggested preparing for potential terrorist events to assure effective response. The response function is largely the focus of the models.

The aforementioned activities represent a very narrow view of how to respond to the threat and actuality of terrorism. The activities do not represent a comprehensive approach to the hazards presented by terrorist violence, although some elements of hazard mitigation and disaster recovery are evident in the policy models. The development of a comprehensive emergency management model for terrorism in its many forms and the assessment of the applicability of the Integrated Emergency Management System model are the tasks here.

A COMPREHENSIVE EMERGENCY MANAGEMENT MODEL FOR TERRORISM

The potential for mass destruction and mass casualty terrorist events, whether sponsored by governments or by nongovernmental groups, strongly suggests that the design of policies and programs to deal with the phenomenon of terrorism should be adequate to the task of preventing or mitigating the effects of such violence, preparing for the range of problems that might result from a terrorist-sponsored disaster, responding effectively to resolve the immediate crisis caused by terrorists and to provide emergency support to the victims, and restoring mimimum life support systems to assure recovery from the effects of such a disaster. The outline of a comprehensive emergency management system based on the four-phase model and the policy intervention models is provided in Table 1.

MITIGATION OF TERRORIST VIOLENCE

The mitigation function may be the major limitation on the development of a comprehensive set of programs. The fragmentation of responsibility among numerous government agencies, quasi-governmental agencies, and nongovernmental entities, ranging from multipurpose government agencies and international organizations to business firms and private humanitarian organizations, complicates the process of responding to the threat of terrorism either to prevent violence altogether or to lessen its effects. The actors perceive and respond to the violent events differently. That was explicit in the development of the models of terrorism in the previous chapter to illustrate some of the interpretations of terrorist violence. In short, international organizations, humanitarian groups, foreign governments, private firms, and other organizations and individuals can perceive their own relationships to the major actors in a number of ways and, thus, can interpret their own responsibility to respond to the threat or actuality of violence.

The principle of international law that sovereign nations have sole legal jurisdiction over and responsibility for events within their own borders and involving their own nationals is only valid in interpreting the actions of those sovereign nations. In reality, domestic political violence, whether sponsored by governments or nongovernmental groups and whether in support of incumbent elites or against, spills over into neighboring nations and increasingly into the broader international community. Humanitarian groups, international organizations, and other foreign interests, moreover, do not necessarily recognize the sanctity of domestic concerns and jurisdictions. External interests can and do

TABLE 1   Emergency Management Functions and Antiterrorism Policy
Interventions

Emergency management functions	Antiterrorism policy interventions
Preparedness	Preparation of response units Planning Development of communication networks Designation of lead agencies Physical security
Mitigation	Obstruction (denial of opportunity to attack most vulnerable targets) Isolation of terrorists from supporters Alteration of terrorists' operational environment (e.g., reduce opportunities to launch large-scale attacks)
Response	Containment of terrorist threat Containment of terrorists' propaganda messages Reassurance of target group Direct response to terrorist demands Retaliation
Recovery	Containment of terrorist threat Restoration of services Counseling of victims and responders Aid to families of victims

Source: Adapted from Waugh (1986).

influence events in a foreign nation as was indicated in the models
of terrorism. International interdependence is social and political,
as well as economic. External audiences represent important
actors in most types of terrorism, in other words.

The mitigation function has to begin with the possibility of
preventing terrorist violence altogether. The literature on antiterrorism policymaking includes many injunctions against giving in

to terrorist demands, i.e., letting terrorists achieve their objectives, because that might encourage further violence. Comparatively little attention is paid to the merits of eliminating the precipitants of terrorist violence, particularly when the terrorists have legitimate grievances against the government or its officials, a segment of society, a business corporation, or another group (Waugh, 1982). One of the assumptions underlying the "civil disorder" model of terrorism is that the precipitants of violence can be removed, i.e., governments can act to eliminate the legitimate grievances of the terrorists. If terrorism is viewed as a frustration-aggression reaction, logic suggests that eliminating the sources of frustration can eliminate the violence (Waugh, 1989). Similarly, if terrorism is viewed as "angry violence" bent on destruction rather than the achievement of a particular political or economic goal, eliminating the causes of that anger should reduce or eliminate the violence (Davies, 1977).

The debate within the General Assembly of the United Nations has focused on the legitimacy of violence used to combat racism, colonialism, imperialism, and other forms of domination suggesting that those conditions themselves constitute terrorism. Notwithstanding the political arguments for or against that broad view of terrorism and the legitimacy of counterterrorism motivated violence, the clear suggestion is that the alleviation of those conditions will reduce the incidence (and legitimacy) of terrorism.

Mitigation programs can also focus on the cultivation of a climate that is hostile to terrorists, thus reducing their opportunity to use violence and increasing the likelihood that they will be identified and captured. The terrorists' operational environment can be made less hospitable through:

1. International treaties that reduce the flow of arms, munitions, monies, and other critical materials to the organization (Bell, 1975: 84-85),
2. Bilateral and multilateral treaties that deny terrorists staging areas outside of the target nation (Huntington, 1962: 26-27),

3. International treaties that outlaw support for terrorist organizations (Wilkinson, 1977: 222, 225), and

4. Bilateral and multilateral treaties that provide for the trial or extradition of terrorists (the principle of *aut punire aut dedere*) (Dinstein, 1975: 165; Wilkinson, 1977: 221-222; Vogler, 1975: 391-399).

Closer to home, the major opportunities for governments to intervene in the process of terrorism, just as they may intervene to reduce other hazards, may focus on structural or engineering approaches and/or regulatory and planning approaches. General actions might include programs to:

1. Identify potential terrorists and the most likely targets of terrorist violence so that resources can be targeted where they will be the most effective in reducing violence;

2. Monitor the vulnerability of potential targets, be they people or facilities, to facilitate preparedness programs;

3. Provide technical assistance to agencies that may have to respond to terrorist events, thus improving response and recovery capabilities (FEMA, 1987);

4. Develop working relationships with individuals, agencies, and jurisdictions that might have to respond to terrorist events, thus cultivating support for mitigation and other emergency management programs (FEMA, 1987);

5. Reduce the availability of arms, explosives, and other materials critical to large scale violence;

6. Monitor and control the movement of people across national borders, particularly suspected terrorists and particularly people traveling to locales that might be targets of terrorist violence;

7. Monitor large transfers of money and thefts of weapons and other supplies that may presage terrorist violence or support terrorist organizations; and,

8. Secure the most likely terrorist targets to deny terrorists the opportunity, or at least to reduce the opportunity, to attack particular persons or facilities.

Certainly the actions above do not exhaust the possibilities for reducing the likelihood of violence. There are hundreds of other possible actions, not all consistent with the civil liberties provided under most democratic regimes, that might prove effective, including increasing intelligence on terrorist operations through infiltration and observation, conducting "head checks" to monitor suspected terrorists in their homes, preventive detention (Wilkinson, 1977: 194), preemptive strikes against terrorists and/or terrorist bases, and so on. Structural approaches may include designing buildings to facilitate security, e.g., restricting access routes into and out of the buildings, designing floorplans to accommodate camera surveillance and/or security patrols, and moving difficult to monitor activities away from public areas. Airport security, for example, was aided significantly when luggage lockers were moved away from the areas with high pedestrian traffic in air terminals, thus reducing the hazard from bombs and reducing risk in boarding areas.

There is also some overlap with the response function in the sense that well-developed programs to contain the threat of violence and the political message that the terrorists are seeking to communicate can lessen the effects of the violence, facilitate recovery, and reassure the targets of the violence. This also suggests that the agency responsible for the mitigation, preparedness, and recovery phases of antiterrorism programs also be very much involved in the response phase. Broader concerns should be represented in the response than the simple resolution of the terrorist event.

The Reality of Mitigation Programs

Mitigation programs are likely to be of extremely low salience in communities that do not perceive that they have a significant risk of being involved directly or indirectly in a terrorist event. Terrorists may choose targets simply because local authorities are not prepared to respond to such violence, so low issue salience may be particularly debilitating for antiterrorism programs.

Locally, too, antiterrorism programs generally lack strong administrative and political constituencies, although police departments usually display some fondness for the kinds of specialized training that may be given to antiterrorist forces whether a real threat exists or not and despite the economic and manpower costs. Antiterrorism programs, of course, gain administrative and political support when administrators and influential publics are threatened or a very large segment of the population perceives danger and demands action.

The greatest resistance to terrorism hazard mitigation programs may be among those concerned about the political, social, economic, and legal implications of regulatory and structural efforts. The most effective ways to reduce terrorist violence may be to outlaw private firearms, regulate strictly the use of explosives, and make it difficult for terrorist organizations to move freely within a society. Few industrialized societies do not strictly regulate the use of explosives and privately owned firearms. The United States has one of the least restrictive policies on firearms and a correspondingly high rate of gun-related crime and political violence. The current debate in the U.S. over the accessibility of military assault rifles is indicative of the problem in regulating activities that might aid terrorist organizations. In some respects, the strong interest group support for continuing to permit such weapons to be purchased by private citizens is similar to the opposition emergency managers frequently encounter when they attempt to employ land-use regulations to mitigate natural hazards. Democratic societies are also generally hesitant to regulate the movement of people within their borders, except when there is a credible threat of violence and the regulation appears justified. Terrorist organizations may, in fact, seek to provoke overreactions by governments as a means of encouraging them to alienate their own popular support through restrictive, repressive measures (Waugh, 1983).

Civil libertarian organizations may be perceived as opponents of effective action against anti-regime forces, but they should also be perceived as proponents of mitigation programs against regime-sponsored terrorism and opponents of overreactions to terrorist threats, i.e., mitigating government counterterrorism measures. Bills of rights and constitutional and statutory guarantees of civil liberties are mitigation efforts. Amnesty International and other humanitarian organizations, as well as multilateral and bilateral human rights agreements, serve that same function within the international community.

Structural mitigation programs may also prove effective, but can tend to be quite expensive. Security precautions, ranging from changes in building design to the use of electronic surveillance equipment, exact economic costs that may outweigh the benefits or, at minimum, are hard to justify given the uncertain risk of terrorism. Terrorists may simply avoid or circumvent structural barriers.

The effectiveness of mitigation efforts is also difficult to measure given that terrorist violence tends to be cyclic and that, despite the common wisdom, there are few indications that particular antiterrorism programs have resulted in significant reductions in the number of terrorist incidents. Some of the exceptions to that generalization, however, include the apparent effectiveness of anti-hijacking measures implemented in the early 1970s. Also, a reduction in Irish Republican Army violence in the mid-1970s has been attributed to the Northern Ireland (Emergency Provisions) Act of 1973 which permitted searches without warrant, detention of suspects, "head checks" to determine the whereabouts of suspected IRA members, and "P-tests" involving random checks on individuals (Wilkinson, 1977: 154). The justifiability of those measures is subject to debate, of course.

The likelihood that terrorism may present very complex technical problems for responding authorities is an important consideration. The problem of developing the right kind of expertise when the risk is impossible to assess with any accuracy is a very real one. Nonetheless, terrorism presents a very elemental problem for society and, fortunately, terrorists have thus far shown greater willingness to wage low-scale wars than they have to use more sophisticated and more destructive methods.

Both the fragmented nature of most modern governmental

systems, both federal and unitary, and the questionable capacities of regional and local governments to respond effectively to large scale violence complicate the development of mitigation programs. Even the unitary governments, like Britain and the Netherlands, have experienced problems in attempting to use national police forces in localized disturbances (Jacobs, 1987a and 1987b, 1990; Hart, 1987). While national authorities, in most cases, are charged with designing mitigation programs, the implementation of those programs, as well as the first response to disaster events, is generally a local responsibility. Similarly, the economic considerations involved in mitigation programs are common to most of the industrialized nations, although for those that have have experienced frequent and highly destructive acts of terrorism presenting real, credible threats to social order and public safety the economic costs may be more easily justified.

The sheer diversity of terrorism-related hazards complicates the design and implementation of mitigation programs. Terrorism can take many forms and it is usually easiest to focus on the major actors involved and their own political and organizational objectives to determine the likeliest locales and intensities of their attacks. Most terrorist organizations have limited reportoires of techniques to influence their targets and other audiences (Waugh, 1983).

PREPAREDNESS FOR TERRORIST VIOLENCE AND DISASTERS

The preparation for a terrorist perpetrated disaster is dependent upon the hazard analysis. Capability assessments, including resource inventories and testing plans, are essentially the same as they might be for a natural disaster. The major difference, however, is in defining the exposure, i.e., identifying all the locales that may be attacked and persons who are at risk and assessing their vulnerability. Terrorists typically choose targets that offer little danger to themselves, so target identification is a major problem unless the political objectives of the terrorists are clearly defined and very specific. But, they also tend to choose targets in areas that permit relatively easy public access and, for foreign terrorists, afford some opportunity to avoid detection before or after an attack. International airports, large cities, major international event sites, resorts, and other areas where foreigners are not conspicuous provide the best opportunities for terrorists to strike, although tightened airport security has certainly reduced the number of attacks on airplanes and terminal facilities since the early 1970s. Nonetheless, the potential for terrorist attacks is still high in such locales and the identification and definition of risk should be sensitive to that potential. Similarly the vulnerability of critical life support systems, such as power, water, communications, and transportation networks, must be considered because of the potential disruption that might result from a terrorist attack.

It may also be possible to anticipate terrorist violence when an event, such as a controversial speaker, a political rally, or the opening of an unpopular business, may precipitate violence. Assessments of both terrorist strengths and objectives can be gained through intelligence gathering, including analyses of past events (e.g., Mickolus, 1978), terrorist personalities (e.g., Hubbard, 1971 ; Kobetz and Cooper, 1978; Clutterbuck, 1975), and terrorist organizations (e.g., Dobson and Payne, 1979) and information provided by private citizens, cooperative governments (e.g., Beall, 1976; Bell, 1975), and defectors.

It might also be anticipated that new and old regimes may misuse the authority of the state to intimidate opposition political parties and/or the news media and, given the high costs of nuclear and conventional warfare, may choose to use terrorist violence to project national power beyond their borders. In comparison to more conventional methods of warfare, terrorism can be inexpensive and more focused politically and easy to support logistically.

Beyond the identification of hazards, a comprehensive preparedness program for terrorism related risk or hazards would include the development of:

1. Operation plans to structure and facilitate the emergency response by police (and/or military) and other public

safety and emergency management personnel, as well as volunteer or emergent groups that will respond to the emergency;

2. An emergency management organization with desig-nated lead agencies, cooperative agreements, and mecha-nisms for liaison and coordination to carry out the plans;

3. A resource management capability recognizing the full range of public, private, and nonprofit sector resources that can be marshalled in an emergency and having the capacity to allocate those resources effectively;

4. Direction and control mechanisms to assure that the lead agencies can effectively guide the emergency response, coordinate efforts, and allocate resources;

5. Emergency communications networks to tie together the emergency management organization;

6. Alert and warning systems to make the public aware of the threat and the need to evacuate or take some other action to reduce danger;

7. Public information channels to keep the public informed so that they can effectively avoid the danger areas and prepare for evacuation if warranted, as well as to assure that the danger is perceived as real and the actions of the authorities are perceived as necessary and credible;

8. Continuity of government to assure consistent and continuing control of the emergency management efforts, as well as to assure the performance of other necessary governmental functions;

9. Shelter protection to provide immediate and adequate housing for affected populations for the duration of an emergency;

10. Evacuation capability to move threatened populations away from the danger prior to disasters;

11. Protective measures to reduce the threat to populations in or near the affected areas;

12. Emergency support services to provide an adequate and timely response to a disaster;

13. Emergency reporting to assure effective monitoring of the situation and appraisal of the emergency response;
14. Training and education programs to assure that emergency personnel are adequately prepared to respond to a potential disaster; and
15. Exercises and drills so that the plans and organizational arrangements can be tested and changed when necessary (adapted from McLoughlin, 1985: 168).

The Reality of Disaster Preparedness

Planning for emergency responses involves a variety of agencies and jurisdictions, thus a fragmented political system presents a number of major coordination problems. Local authorities are likely to be the first responders to a terrorist event and they must be involved in the planning phase and have lead roles in the response plan. The coordination of multiagency responses may be the single most pressing task for emergency managers and it is most effectively accomplished long before a disaster strikes.

The preparedness function, too, generally suffers from the lack of strong administrative and political constituencies. At the community level there is little support for a well-developed response capacity, until a disaster strikes. That is no less true of terrorism-related preparations than it is of other kinds of disaster preparation. While there may be a very capable police force with appropriate training to respond to terrorist events, the likelihood of having a broader focused emergency management program is much less.

An adequate operational capability will also likely require significant infusions of national funds and technical assistance to increase local government capacity. In large measure, such infusions are taking place in the U.S. and other developed nations in terms of training exercises and the transfer of antiterrorism technologies, but it is uncertain whether the transfers are reaching all the jurisdictions that may need them. In the preparedness function, too, the effectiveness of programs may be hard to establish without realistic tests, but the costs are more easily measured.

Local self-reliance is not a realistic option given the range of potential terrorist crises. Preparedness efforts should accommodate worst case scenarios to the extent practicable and few local governments have the wherewithal to respond to large scale disasters of any kind without outside assistance.

RESPONDING TO TERRORIST EVENTS

While responses to terrorist events generally focus on the police or military response to the terrorists themselves, a more comprehensive response such events would generally include resolving the crisis if it is continuing, reducing the impact of the violence on the targets and other audiences, reducing the danger to public health and safety, and providing immediate care to those injured. An emergency response most often is carried out under circumstances that are characterized by: (1) risk; (2) uncertainty; (3) ambiguity or fluidity; (4) competition/conflict among values; (5) an action orientation; (6) time constraints; (7) communications limitations; (8) variations in data/information; and, (9) potentially dire and very political consequences (Lewis, 1988: 167-68). In continuing terrorist events (e.g., kidnappings, barricade and hostage cases, and threats of violence), those characteristics would manifest themselves as very hazardous conditions involving ambiguous situational and environmental variables requiring quick action, although not all policy options will be acceptable given the cultural and political values of the community, region, nation, or world community. To say that some cultures have value systems more consonant with the use of terrorist violence begs the issue. To say that some cultures are predisposed toward certain political responses to terrorists also begs the issue. Cultural values are in fact principal determinants of the definitions of terrorism and, as such, influence both the willingness to mitigate and prepare for terrorist violence and the character of the response to such violence.

The Reality of Emergency Response

Issue salience is not generally a problem in responding to disasters precipitated by terrorists, although the public can be slow to recognize catastrophic events that do not develop quickly, such as those being caused by acid rain and a depleted ozone layer in the outer atmosphere. In many respects, it is easier to find support for emergency responses than it is for disaster mitigation and preparedness efforts. There are ready political and administrative constituencies for such action. That is no less true of terrorist-sponsored events than it is of other kinds of disasters although there may be some differences in the interpretation of the events, particularly if the official government interpretation is challenged. Support for particular kinds of emergency response also may be lacking. Terrorists may, in fact, seek to provoke an overreaction to their violence to discredit the actions of the government (Fromkin, 1975: 131; Rapoport, 1971 : 62; Jenkins, 1975: 17; Evans, 1979 : 31-32; Grabosky, 1979: 61; Waugh, 1983). Governments, too, may use terrorist violence as an excuse to abridge civil liberties and to reduce opposition (Waugh, 1982).

The constituencies for action against "revolutionary," "civil disorder," and other forms of nonstate terrorism are usually the military and national security establishments and the domestic police. In the case of terrorism directed against foreign nationals and / or facilities, international terrorism that has spilled over into an otherwise uninvolved state, the constituencies for action may be foreign governments and international organizations rather than domestic administrative and political groups. Similarly, the constituencies for action against state-sponsored violence may include international human rights organizations, as well as domestic human rights and political opposition groups. Whatever the perspective on the proper response, terrorism normally evokes a strong public reaction when it is identified.

The public is generally more supportive of regulatory actions that are credible responses to identifiable hazards. The crisis faced by the Israeli government in the late 1980s when international and domestic audiences perceived that police and military forces were overreacting to Palestinian protests is a case in point. Palestinian members of the police force resigned in large numbers and some Jewish military personnel resigned in protest as well.

Effective public information and warning systems, too, are essential to gaining public support and compliance in the emergency response (Perry, 1985).

The fragmented governmental system may be the principal obstacle to effective emergency response. It is often difficult to resolve the question of jurisdiction prior to a disaster when the exact location of the event cannot be predicted. Terrorist events may take place almost anywhere and certainly terrorists generally try to be unpredictable in their choice of targets. It can be argued that terrorists who can openly challenge government authority or the weight of public opinion have moved beyond the usual definitions of "terrorism" and are engaged in civil war or totalitarian oppression. In the American case, the fragmented governmental arrangement means that ultimate jurisdiction over a terrorist caused disaster may lie with a small community's public safety apparatus, rather than with state or federal police or military forces. Societies with unitary forms of government may have fewer jurisdiction problems, particularly if the central government is assigned principal jurisdiction over cases of terrorism, but coordination with local authorities and the speed of response are major problems (e.g., see, Jacobs, 1990). In either system, the fiscal, administrative, and political resources available to the affected community in its response may be very quickly outstripped by events. As will be examined later, it cannot be assumed that trained and experienced antiterrorism forces and related emergency management programs can be mobilized quickly enough and have the legal authority to intervene in the event without first being invited to do so. While many communities do have special police units trained somewhat for hostage and antiterrorist responses, it is uncertain that the expertise is either adequate to the task of responding to a wide range of possible disasters or lesser crises or sufficiently developed to respond to a major catastrophe. Radiological and biological disasters certainly would present major problems.

Effective preparedness efforts, including agreements on jurisdiction and joint action, can reduce the coordination problems, but the very nature of emergency responses can complicate those relations. This is not to argue that the coordination of effective responses is impossible; rather it is to argue that coordination can be accomplished only with very great difficulty. In large measure those problems are a product of the dilemma caused by the centralization of technical expertise and the localized nature of disasters, as well as by fragmented jurisdictional responsibilities.

RECOVERING FROM TERRORIST-SPONSORED DISASTERS

The discussion of antiterrorism policies and programs seldom focuses on the recovery phase of managing the events. That may be due to the inexperience of most jurisdictions in dealing with large scale, mass casualty terrorist events. Most nations tend to rely on ad hoc national recovery programs when major disasters outstrip the capacities of local authorities, although many developing nations have to rely on international disaster assistance for both emergency response and recovery efforts (with little attention to mitigation and preparedness, except to the extent that major disasters may lead to the implementation of such programs as part of the recovery effort and utilizing the infusion of outside funds and expertise). The restoration of life support services is a minimal recovery effort.

Terrorist events have caused large scale homelessness as people have fled or been removed from threatened areas and food shortages as crops and storage facilities have been destroyed or food has been diverted from local use. Those are familiar scenarios for international humanitarian agencies. Recovery efforts, in those cases, are often complicated by the persistence of violence, requiring the resolution of political and economic conflicts before recovery programs can be fully implemented. The victims are major actors in the conflict and their suffering can be used as a weapon by the competing factions, be they governments or challengers to incumbent authorities.

The Reality of Disaster Recovery

Recovery programs usually enjoy wide public and official support, although not all may agree on the form recovery should take. Consensus on the need to act often breaks down during the recovery phase as political and administrative constituencies, as well as the public as a whole, see the potential for gain (or loss) and begin pursuing their own self-interests rather than a more generalized public good. In the case of terrorist events, many political factions can gain or lose as a result of a major action. The aftermath of disaster provides the opportunity for challenging political forces to supplant the authority of the regime in power or for regimes to discredit their opposition or penetrate the strongholds of competing elites. The political nature of terrorism, quite apart from the politics of responding to its threat, certainly complicates the emergency manager's operational environment. Political values, as suggested in the models, may be seen as overriding the values of human life and property loss.

Recovery efforts often exceed the administrative and economic capacities of local authorities and that is no less true of programs implemented in the aftermath of terrorist-spawned disasters. Here, too, fragmented government responsibility for designing, implementing, administering, and financing recovery programs can cause problems. The history of disaster legislation in the U.S. suggests that action taken in response to specific disasters often provides little foundation for responding to the next disaster (May and Williams, 1986).

The aftermath of disaster, too, is characterized by the assignment of blame for the disaster itself, the extent of the damage, and/or the failure to prepare for, mitigate the effects of, and respond to the disaster effectively. The Soviet government's decision to seek out and prosecute the builders responsible for the poor construction of buildings in Armenia, is a case in point. Structural collapses caused hundreds, if not thousands, of deaths in the Armenian earthquake of 1988.

The great advantage in implementing recovery programs is that disasters give the programs credibility and salience. Despite political, economic, and administrative obstacles, humanitarian interests demand action.

CONCLUSIONS: THE NEED FOR A COMPREHENSIVE EMERGENCY MANAGEMENT PROGRAM FOR TERRORIST-SPONSORED DISASTERS

Most of the same emergency management concerns that characterize reactions to natural and technological hazards and disaster also are present in government reactions to terrorist threats and disasters. In both cases, there is a need to mitigate the effects of, prepare for, respond to, and recover from the disasters - or to be ready to do so when such events occur. In that regard, the four-phase emergency management model has some utility for antiterrorism programs. The emergency management activities mentioned in Chapter 2, therefore, may provide some guidance in the development of an effective set of programs to address terrorism-related hazards and disasters.

The discussion has also pointed out the need for a lead agency for the terrorism emergency management program, as well as the difficulty coordinating such a program. To establish appropriate mitigation programs, including the assessment of risk, the agency needs to have a broad perspective on the violence and its potential effects. Similarly, the agency should have broad administrative and political responsibilities, as well as fiscal resources, to develop, implement, and maintain a broad range of preparedness programs.

To coordinate the emergency response, such an agency should have a clearly defined set of responsibilities. While having sole jurisdiction over terrorist events may facilitate operations, that is not a likely prospect given the number of agencies that may be involved and the variety of forms that terrorism may take. No agency would have enough technical expertise to address every type of emergency and problems are created when the agency with jurisdiction and the agency with the necessary expertise are not the same (Waugh, 1990). More realistically, the emergency management agency should be clearly identified as the lead agency with effective mechanisms to coordinate the operations of all responding agencies. In a federal system, that would require effective intragovernmental and intergovernmental coordination.

It is perhaps less important that there be a clearly designated lead agency for the recovery phase following a disaster. But, it is essential that the agencies responsible for recovery be involved in the earlier phases to assure that the overall program is effective. Indeed, the effectiveness of recovery and reconstruction is a measure of the effectiveness of the whole emergency management program. That is no less true of terrorism-related emergency management programs than it is of natural and technological disaster-related programs.

In terms of the applicability of the Integrated Emergency Management System to terrorist inspired disasters, it does suggest the need for a lead emergency management agency to coordinate the development of hazard analyses, capability assessments, and emergency operations plans, as well as implementing, maintaining, and evaluating the mitigation and emergency response programs. Such an agency would need considerable expertise and funding to keep the system operating. The extent to which such an all-hazard program would be adequate to the tasks that might be demanded of it in an terrorist-related disaster is difficult to judge. It is still uncertain that such a program can be an effective answer to the threats posed by a variety of natural and technological disasters. As an alternative to the uncoordinated complex of policies and programs that address specific disaster-types, such as hurricanes and floods, the IEMS model appears promising.

The problem with applying such a framework to a government's antiterrorism efforts is that military and law enforcement agencies typically have principal jurisdiction over terrorist events, particularly during the response phase of an emergency operation. As was suggested by the models of terrorism offered earlier, the actions of those responding agencies are generally based on a particular set of assumptions about the violence that may or may not be accurate. Those assumptions will also affect the decisions made during the response and may also affect the design of the mitigation, preparedness, and recovery efforts. These are the issues that will be addressed in the final chapter.

REFERENCES

Marshall D. Beall (1976) "Hostage Negotiations," *Military Police Law Enforcement Journal* 3 (Fall).

J. Bowyer Bell (1975) *Transnational Terror* (Washington, DC: American Enterprise Institute).

James P. Bennett and Thomas L. Saaty (1979) "Terrorism: Patterns for Negotiation --- A Case Study Using Hierarchies and Holarchies," in *Terrorism: Threat, Reality, Response,* edited by Robert Kupperman and Darrell Trent (Stanford, Calif.: Hoover Institution Press).

Richard Clutterbuck (1975) *Living With Terrorism* (New Rochelle, N.Y.: Arlington House Publishers).

Congressional Research Service, Library of Congress (1984) *Information Technology for Emergency Management* (Report prepared for the Subcommittee on Investigations and Oversight, Committee on Science and Technology, U.S. House of Representatives), Washington, DC: US Government Printing Office, October 9.

Thomas B. Davies (1977) *Feedback Processes and International Terrorism,* Unpublished Ph.D. Dissertation, Florida State University (Ann Arbor, Michigan: University Microfilms).

Yoram Dinstein (1975) "Terrorism and War of Liberation: An Israeli Perspective of the Arab-Israeli Conflict," in *International Terrorism and Political Crime,* edited by M. Cherif Bassiouni (Springfield, Ill.: Charles C. Thomas Publishers).

Christopher Dobson and Ronald Payne (1979) *The Terrorists: Their Weapons, Leaders and Tactics* (New York: Facts on File, Inc.).

Ernest Evans (1979) *Calling a Truce to Terror* (Westport, Conn.: Greenwood Press).

Federal Emergency Management Agency (1987) *Integrated Emergency Management System: Mitigation Program Development Guidance,* Washington, DC: FEMA-122, March.

David Fromkin (1975) "The Strategy of Terrorism," *Foreign Affairs* (July): 683-98.

P.N. Grabosky (1979) "The Urban Context of Political Terrorism," in *The Politics of Terrorism,* edited by Michael Stohl (New York: Marcel Dekker).

Paul 't Hart (1987) "Pattern of Crisis Decision Making: The Heyzel Stadium Tragedy," Paper presented at the Workshop on Crisis Decision Making: An International Perspective, International Institute of Administrative Sciences, Brussels, Belgium, December.

David B. Hubbard (1971) *The Skyjacker: His Flights of Fancy* (New York: Macmillan).

Samuel P. Huntington (1962) "Patterns of Violence in World Politics," in *Changing Patterns of Military Politics*, pp. 17-50, edited by Samuel P. Huntington (Glencoe, NY: Free Press).

Brian D. Jacobs (1987a) "The Brixton Riots: London 1981," Paper presented at a Workshop on Crisis Management: An International Perspective, International Institute for Administrative Sciences, Brussels, Belgium, December.

Brian D. Jacobs (1987b) "Relations Between Different Levels of Government," Presentation at the Conference on Crisis Management: An International Perspective, International Institute for Administrative Sciences/Faculty of the Catholic University of Mons, Mons, Belgium, December 15-16.

Brian D. Jacobs (1990) "Controlling Terrorism in the United Kingdom," in *Antiterrorism Policy: An International Comparison*, edited by William L. Waugh, Jr., and Jane P. Sweeney (London and Brussels: Routledge).

Brian Michael Jenkins (1975) *International Terrorism: A New Mode of Conflict* (Los Angeles: Crescent Publications).

Richard W. Kobetz and H.H.A. Cooper (1978) *Target Terrorism: Providing Protective Services* (Gaithersburg, Md.: International Association of Chiefs of Police).

Ralph G. Lewis (1988) "Management Issues in Emergency Response," pp. 163-79 in *Managing Disaster: Strategies and Policy Perspectives*, edited by Louise K. Comfort (Durham, NC: Duke University Press).

Peter J. May and Walter Williams (1986) *Disaster Policy Implementation: Managing Programs Under Shared Governance* (New York and London: Plenum Press).

David McLoughlin (1985) "A Framework for Integrated Emergency Management," *Public Administration Review* (January): 165-172.

Edward Mickolus (1978) "Trends in Transnational Terrorism," pp. 44-73 in *International Terrorism in the Contemporary World*, edited by Marius H. Livingston (Westport, Conn.: Greenwood Press).

Ronald W. Perry (1985) *Comprehensive Emergency Management: Evacuating Threatened Populations* (Greenwich, Conn.: JAI Press).

David C. Rapoport (1971) *Assassination and Terrorism* (Toronto: Canadian Broadcasting Corporation).

Theo Vogler (1975) "Perspectives on Extradition and Terrorism," in *International Terrorism and Political Crimes*, edited by M. Cherif Bassiouni (Springfield, Ill.: Charles C. Thomas).

William L. Waugh, Jr. (1982) *International Terrorism: How Nations Respond to Terrorists* (Chapel Hill, NC: Documentary Publications)

William L. Waugh, Jr. (1983) "The Values in Violence: Organizational and Political Objectives of Terrorist Groups," *Conflict Quarterly* (Summer): 5-19.

William L. Waugh, Jr. (1986) "Integrating the Policy Models of Terrorism and Emergency Management," *Policy Studies Review* (December): 287-300.

William L. Waugh, Jr. (1987) "The Administrative Challenge of the Iranian Hostage Crisis," Paper presented at the Workshop on Crisis Management: An International Perspective, Institute of Administrative Sciences, Brussels, Belgium, December.

William L. Waugh, Jr. (1989) "Informing Policy and Administration: A Comparative Perspective on Terrorism," *International Journal of Public Administration* 12 (January).

William L. Waugh, Jr. (1990) "Hurricanes," in *Emergency Management Handbook*, edited by William L. Waugh, Jr., and Ronald John Hy (Westport, Conn.: Greenwood Press).

Paul Wilkinson (1977) *Terrorism and the Liberal State* (New York: Wiley).

Chapter 5

TERRORISM POLICIES AND PROGRAMS IN THE U.S.

INTRODUCTION

When President Reagan entered office in January of 1981, as the long and politically embarrassing hostage ordeal in Teheran drew to a close, his inaugeral address promised that terrorists would received "swift and effective retribution" from the U.S. government for their violence. Notwithstanding that naive promise and despite the bluster and threats that continued to characterize official statements during the remainder of the Reagan Administration, a more effective American policy emerged as policymaking became more pragmatic and less ideological. Still, as the journalists Martin and Walcott have characterized it (1988), the initial actions of the Reagan Administration were an overreaction to the threat and were based on "ignorance and blind anti-communism." The lack of understanding of the terrorist threat likely alienated international support for U.S. actions and did little to alleviate the problem itself. Clearly, as the Administration wore on, however, the rhetoric became more tempered and the policy more pragmatic. Indeed, the apparent adoption of a law enforcement, rather than a military, orientation in antiterrorism policy indicates a fundamental change in how terrorism was viewed. The evolution of that policy and the structure of current U.S. programs will illustrate how an emergency management framework can be used to respond to the threat of terrorism. Indeed, changing the perspective on terrorism may permit more effective action by American officials.

The problem of terrorism has received considerable attention in the U.S., despite the relatively low incidence of domestic and international terrorist events within American borders. Warren A. Bradish of the U.S. Army's Counterintelligence and Security Division (Headquarters, FORSCOM) at Fort McPherson, Georgia, indicated in a 1986 presentation that "more than 150 specific activities to combat terrorism now are carried out by various federal departments and agencies." He went on to cite estimated expenditures for those activities in 1985 alone to be around $2 billion, with the expenditures for new construction and structural modifications over a five-year period to be approximately $2.7 billion.

Several explanations have been offered for that level of attention. First, and perhaps most importantly, while terrorist violence is still relatively uncommon, there is a very high potential for mass destruction terrorism due to the fragility of modern transportation, communication, energy, water, and other critical networks. U.S. law enforcement and antiterrorism agencies have, in fact, already had some first-hand experience with nuclear and biological threats (see, e.g., Crabtree, 1985). There is some disagreement concerning the value of mass casualty events to terrorist organizations. The Western European experience with nihilistic terrorist groups did not include mass casualty and mass destruction events, but that experience did demonstrate that terrorists might be willing to launch large scale attacks and intentionally to inflict high levels of destruction and mass casualties. Given the modern technologies of war and the relatively unsophisticated technologies necessary to disrupt society, such violence is certainly possible.

Second, there is also the fear that Americans will continue to be preferred targets for foreign terrorists. If terrorist strategy is to win domestic or international support, it makes more sense to choose victims who may not elicit as much sympathy as more familiar victims might and, thus, may not alienate the terrorists' own popular support. It may be easier to attack Americans because they symbolize many of the ills that have been visited on the developing nations and many of the frustrations felt by opposition groups in the more developed nations. Americans may not be seen as sympathetic figures by foreign publics, in other words (Richter and Waugh, 1986). Much the same may be true of attacks on other foreign tourists, business people, and officials, particularly where historical animosities exist.

Americans and other Westerners may also be seen as attractive targets in a symbolic way, because of their governments' international alliances and/or ideological orientations. For example, in May of 1989, the Speaker of the Iranian Parliament, Hashemi Rafsanjani, called upon Palestinians to kill five Westerners for every Palestinian killed by the Israelis. He went on to say: "It isn't so hard to kill Americans or Frenchmen, because they're all over the globe. It's a bit difficult to kill Israelis, because there aren't as many of them around in other parts of the world" (*Atlanta Journal and Constitution*, May 6, 1989). Rafsanjani urged attacks on Americans, Frenchmen, and Britons as an effective way to influence Israeli policy. Despite his recantation a week later, Rafsanjani's point had been made. Westerners are easy targets and, as victims, amplify the political threat.

As long as the U.S. remains a leading state in international affairs, Americans will remain attractive and easy targets. That situation is not likely to change in the near future, although a less strident American foreign policy may be viewed as less of a challenge to foreign terrorists. Moreover, to the extent that successful attacks on American citizens and facilities may become measures of terrorist capacity and power, the risk to Americans will remain high.

Indeed, the statistics for 1980 indicate that Americans or American property were targets in approximately 40% of the incidences of international terrorism throughout the world, with ten Americans being killed and 94 injured (Martin and Walcott, 1988: 46). In terms of the location of terrorist attacks, however, U.S. State Department has calculated that of the 782 incidents of international terrorism (resulting in 800 deaths and 1200 other casualties) occurring in 1985 only .5% or one in 200 occurred in North America (U.S. Department of State, 1986). That latter statistic may in fact be quite important. James E. Winkates at the U.S. Air Force's Air War College suggests that the high incidence of terrorist violence against Americans outside of the U.S. may have reinforced the notion that terrorism is a national security or foreign policy problem, rather than a law enforcement or internal political problem as it is viewed in much of Western Europe (1989). Both sets of numbers are based on a very broad definition of what is international terrorism, however.

Domestic terrorism is another matter. While the incidence of domestic political violence has been relatively low in comparison with some other Western democracies and declining in the 1980's, there has been an increase in right-wing violence in recent years. Here, too, the definitional ambiguities create confusion. For example, much of American political violence is simply defined as criminal activity and subject to the assumptions inherent in the law enforcement model described earlier. Attacks on government facilities are termed political, as are the attacks of left-wing organizations on private businesses; but, attacks by right-wing organizations on women's clinics are generally termed criminal and not warranting a federal response unless they involve bombs. The violence of right-wing organizations like the Ku Klux Klan, for example, is increasingly recognized as terrorism, but the government has not been willing to brand the group itself as terrorist and all members as accomplices in the organization's violent acts. Notwithstanding those biases, law enforcement agencies appear to be giving greater attention to the violent threats posed by right-wing extremist groups and the U.S. State Department has paid greater attention to the violence of right-wing extremists in other parts of the world. The emphasis on human rights was a *cause celebre* of the U.S. State Department during the Carter Administration. While finding somewhat less support in the Reagan Administration and less certain support in the Bush Administration, human rights does remain, at least to some extent, a central concern of American foreign policy.

It must also be noted that the business of combatting terrorism has grown considerably since the early 1970's, with firms such as Risks International, Inc., in Alexandria, Virginia, providing sophisticated risk assessments to the private firms and government agencies willing to pay. Dozens of such firms, many employing former military and intelligence agency personnel, have undoubtedly contributed to the high salience of the issue and may well have a significant influence on the definition of the problem. The quality of the risk assessments and antiterrorism training provided by such firms varies considerably.

The strength of conservative political interests in the Congress and other structures of American government in recent years has also had a significant impact on recent policies. The ideological blinders that affected executive branch antiterrorism efforts during the Reagan Administration, as noted by Martin and Walcott (1988), also affected Congressional efforts. Bills were introduced in the Congress to permit a major expansion of military and civilian law enforcement operations against known and suspected terrorists. The bills stopped just short of approving assassinations of suspected terrorists. Given that most of the bills were in response to particular terrorist events and proposed during the height of the public's concern about terrorist violence, more considered proposals found little support. That has been the context of recent American antiterrorism policymaking.

As will be suggested here, the development of current policies and the design of multi-jurisdictional responses have been shaped largely by the violence of left-wing domestic groups in the 1960's and the national liberation movements of the post-war period. As mentioned earlier, one of those biases has been the propensity at the national level to view terrorism as a national security, rather than a law enforcement, problem. In short, the thesis is that there are built-in biases in American antiterrorism policies that affect the way that the problem of terrorism is addressed and the effectiveness of the policies and programs. Biases certainly are not unusual characteristics of policymaking, but they are important in understanding the issue and how it has been addressed (or not addressed).

The policies and programs of the United States will also be fit into the frameworks for emergency management, the design of current policies will be explained by the models of terrorism on which they were based, and the comprehensiveness of the policies when measured against the Integrated Emergency Management System model will be examined. Those are the tasks to be addressed here. First, however, we must examine the definitions of terrorism used by U.S. government agencies and officials and the general structure of American antiterrorism programs.

DEFINING TERRORISM

In many respects, American antiterrorism policymaking has been characterized by a search for a legal definition of terrorism. The definitional confusion among U.S. officials and agencies has been noted before (Waugh, 1982) and does not require reiteration. It is useful to note, however, that the definitions used by the U.S. State Department have changed significantly in the past ten to fifteen years. In 1978, for example, Ambassador Anthony C.E. Quainton, of the State Department's Office for Combatting Terrorism identified the following definition of international terrorism as the one most widely used in the U.S. government:

> ... the threat or use of violence for political purposes when such action is intended to influence the attitude and behavior or a target group wider than its immediate victims and its ramifications transcend national boundaries (1978).

That is essentially the same definition as the one used by the Central Intelligence Agency at that time, although the CIA version went on to qualify how the violence's "ramifications may transcend national boundaries" (see, e.g., Milbank, 1976). A 1986

U.S. Department of State publication uses new, broader definitions of terrorism and international terrorism:

> *Terrorism* is premeditated, politically motivated violence perpe-
> trated against noncombatant targets by subnational groups or
> clandestine state agents, usually intended to influence an
> audience.
>
> *International Terrorism* is terrorism involving citizens or territory
> of more than one country (1988).

In some respects the definitions are similar. The 1985 definition, however, specifies that the targets are "noncombatants," the
groups are "subnational or clandestine state agents," and the
intent to influence a broader audience is the usual, but not
necessarily a required, qualification. The 1986 definitions are very
much broader and legalistic than the earlier one and would
certainly encompass asylum-motivated hijackings and other less
focused forms of violence. The definition of international terrorism is so broad, in fact, that acts of domestic terrorism that
spillover into another state or, presumably, involve a foreign
national even in a peripheral way can be termed "international."
Also, more overt state actions may not fall within the parameters
of the 1986 definition. Interestingly, the bombing of the Marine
barracks in Beirut on October 23, 1983, that resulted in the deaths
of 241 U.S. military personnel, would not fit that definition of
terrorism if those personnel are defined as combatants. Indeed, a
retired military officer writing in *Army* magazine has suggested
that the bombing was an act of "unconventional warfare," an act
of war, rather than an act of terrorism (Simpson, 1984). He
contends that the installation was a military one and the
"peacekeeping" forces were involved in the conflict and thus not
noncombatants. Terroristic acts are common, if not fundamental,
elements in modern warfare as evidenced by current nuclear
strategies supporting attacks on enemy nations' population
centers and modern strategies of subconventional psychological
warfare. At minimum, it can be argued, the U.S. Marine detach-
ment was simply too close to an on-going civil war and the troops
became casualties of that war.

By contrast, a 1985 Federal Bureau of Investigation definition specifies that:

> *Terrorism* is the unlawful use of force or violence against persons or property to intimidate or coerce a government, the civilian population, or any segment thereof, in furtherance of political or social objectives (FBI, 1988).

The FBI definition focuses on the targets of terrorist violence and the political objectives of the terrorists. It, too, is quite broad. Without making too much of the differences in the definitions, it would appear that the development of a conceptualization of terrorism amenable to the identification and classification of events and groups and the analysis of event, typical of the earlier definitions, has given way to finding a legal definition that will facilitate antiterrorism lawmaking. The 1985 Congressional concurrent resolution condemning the murder of a Drug Enforcement Agency official as an act of terrorism, however, confuses the issue somewhat because of its blurring of the distinctions between political and nonpolitical criminal activities. To the extent that national policymakers are finding law enforcement responses to terrorism somewhat effective the distinctions may become even more blurred.

What is suggested here is that the definitions of terrorism on which current U.S. policies are based are still not clear. There is still the tendency to label many kinds of events as acts of terrorism when it is politically useful to do so and to label some acts of terrorism as simple criminality when sympathies do not lie with the victims.

THE ORGANIZATIONAL FRAMEWORK

Responsibility for acts of domestic terrorism, including the kinds of "spillover terrorism" that have little to do with the United States except for occurring within its jurisdiction (Waugh, 1982), rests primarily with local law enforcement agencies. The level of preparation for potential terrorist violence, particularly catastrophic events, ranges from virtually none to very sophisticated programs. New York City, for example, has an Emergency Control Board, a policymaking body under the direction of the Police Commissioner and consisting of the Director of Operations, the deputy mayors, heads of other relevant agencies, and representatives from such private and nonprofit sector organizations as the Red Cross and the utilities. The City's Office of Civil Preparedness is responsible for disaster planning and coordination and an Emergency Coordinating Section, made up of high level department managers, provides liaison between the emergency management organization and city departments. The City's Emergency Management Plan provides guidelines and procedures, including contingency manuals, for a city-wide emergency response. A Phase I emergency mobilizes the Office of Civil Preparedness (OCP) to monitor the situation and provide for call-ups of emergency personnel and 24-hour work schedules. A Phase II emergency prompts the OCP to mobilize the appropriate Emergency Control Board (ECB) liaisons. A Phase III emergency requires that the ECB representatives report to the Emergency Management Center to direct and control emergency operations. Contingency plans for blackouts, mobilization of personnel, air support, hazardous materials, evacuation, and other frequently required emergency operations are ready for implementation if warranted. During a Phase III emergency, only the mayor and the director and deputy director of the Office of Civil Preparedness are authorized to speak for the City (U.S. House of Representatives, 1984). Despite the sophistication of the preparations in New York City, including the computer and telecommunications networks that support the emergency management system, there are gaps in the plans and known problems in implementation (see, e.g., Sylves and Pavlak, 1989). Notwithstanding those weaknesses, the New York City emergency management system is exceptionally well-developed. Coupled with a police department with considerable experience handling hostage, arson, bombing, and other terrorism-type incidences, the City can bring considerable resources to bear on terrorist-sponsored disasters.

New York City represents the exception rather than the rule for local government emergency management capabilities, however.

When local authorities request assistance or the acts involve crimes over which the federal government has jurisdiction (such as bombings, bank robberies, or kidnappings), the Federal Bureau of Investigation can become the principal responder. Exceptions occur when the acts involve aerial hijackings or attacks on specially protected groups, such as diplomats and invited guests of the national government.

Specific responsibility for responding to potential and actual acts of terrorism depends upon the likely targets. The Department of Justice, through the Federal Bureau of Investigation (FBI), is the lead agency for domestic terrorism and the U.S. Department of State is the lead agency for international terrorism. Within the National Security Council (NSC), interagency groups (IGs), composed of representatives of the Senior Interagency Group (i.e., the Director of the CIA, the President's National Security advisor, the Deputy Secretary of Defense, the Deputy Secretary of State, Chairman of the Joint Chiefs of Staff, the Deputy Attorney General, the Director of the FBI, and the Director of the National Security Agency) and other invited participants address specific policy areas. The FBI representative chairs all IG meetings dealing with counterintelligence and representatives of the State Department and the Department of Justice chair meetings dealing with international terrorism (depending upon whether it occurs in the U.S. or outside)(CIA, n.d.)

To reduce jurisdictional confusion, i.e., the chronic "turf" battles that typify decisionmaking in international events, National Security Directive 30 (with addendum) established the Terrorist Incident Working Group to coordinate agency efforts through the NSC. Emergency Support Teams coordinate responses with a Joint Special Operations Command overseeing actual operations overseas (Martin and Walcott, 1988). At issue has been the use of the National Security Council as an operational vehicle, particularly after the scandal surrounding Lt. Colonel Oliver North and the trading of arms to Iran for hostages in the mid-1980's and the heavy handedness of the NSC in the intercept of the EgyptAir flight carrying Abu Abbas and the Achille Lauro hijackers in 1985. President Reagan had created an Interdepartmental Group on Terrorism, reporting through the Secretary of State, to coordinate national efforts (Quainton, 1983), but jurisdictional problems remained.

A commission established by President Reagan and chaired by Vice-President Bush recommended in 1988 that the NSC assume responsibility for coordinating antiterrorism activities and some functions were shifted before President Reagan left office. There was some interest among members of the commission in establishing a single agency responsible for responding to terrorism, but that was not done despite some reshuffling of responsibilities. Presidential Executive Order 12656 (see Appendix), signed by President Reagan on November 18, 1988, for example, assigned primary responsibility for national security preparedness policy, including responses to catastrophic (and, thereby, national security-threatening) terroristic events, to the National Security Council. The role of the Federal Emergency Management Agency in such events was reduced to providing advice to the NSC regarding the status of preparedness programs and coordinating the emergency preparedness efforts of other involved agencies (*Weekly Compilation of Presidential Documents*, November 21, 1988).

Depending on the nature of the target, other agencies may have primary responsibility. For example, the U.S. Marshals Service provides security to all federal courts. The Federal Aviation Administration (FAA) has responsibility for airports and aircraft, although security is largely provided by the air carriers and airport authorities themselves with the FAA providing oversight and technical assistance. Similarly, while the Department of Energy has responsibility for most government nuclear facilities and materials and the Nuclear Regulatory Agency has responsibility for all commercial nuclear facilities, powerplants themselves are responsible for screening employees and providing physical security as part of the licensing process (GAO, 1983; Farrell, 1983).

The Federal Protective Service (FPS), part of the General Services Administration, has responsibility for securing most federal buildings. Following the bombing of the U.S. Capitol in 1983, the FPS closed many of the federal buildings in downtown Washington to the public and increased security in most federal buildings. The measures ranged from installing metal detectors and posting guards in high risk areas to the consolidation of agency offices to facilitate security.

Some potential targets fall through the jurisdictional cracks, however. Hugh W. Stephens at the University of Houston, for example, has noted jurisdictional problems that make it unclear which agency or agencies have the responsibility to protect American maritime facilities, including docks, off-shore oil platforms, and other facilities. The U.S. Coast Guard can control movements in ports and is responsible for developing antiterrorism contingency plans, based on recent amendments to the Ports and Waterways Safety Act of 1972 following the Achille Lauro hijacking. It is also responsible for responding to off-shore oil platform emergencies and attacks on U.S. shipping and facilities beyond the state's off-shore jurisdictions. The capacity of the FBI to respond to off-shore emergencies is questionable, as are the capacities of state and local law enforcement authorities to respond. Responsibility to respond to terrorist attacks in on-shore facilities is somewhat clearer, but jurisdictional overlaps would likely create confusion (Stephens, 1988).

Jurisdiction is certainly clearer in cases of international terrorism outside of the U.S. The Office of the Ambassador-at-Large for Counterterrorism is the Department of State's principal antiterrorism arm. In terms of threats to overseas facilities, the Bureau of Diplomatic Security was created in November of 1985, after the bombing of the Beirut Embassy annex, to reduce the fragmentation of departmental antiterrorism efforts. The new bureau took over responsibility for the Security Enhancement Program established in 1980 following attacks on American embassies in Pakistan, Libya, and Iran. The bureau also absorbed the Special Programs and Liaison office, the Office of Security, and the Office of Counter-Terrorism and Emergency Planning. Interagency coordination has been accomplished through the Overseas

Security Policy Group, established in 1982, although conflict between State and other involved agencies, including the U.S. Information Agency and the U.S. Agency for International Development, has been a continuing problem (GAO, 1986). The implementation of the Omnibus Diplomatic Security and Anti-Terrorism Act of 1986 has been slow, for example. Section 604, requiring coordination among the Department of State, Department of Defense, Department of Energy, Arms Control and Disarmament Agency, and Nuclear Regulatory Agency, has been difficult to implement because of differing agency priorities and objectives (GAO, 1988).

If a military response is contemplated, the Department of Defense takes a lead role. The Navy's Seal Team 6 and the Army's Delta Force are the designated response units. The American public became familiar with the Delta Force during the failed Iran rescue in April of 1980. It was created in 1977 after the Israelis' Entebbe rescue. In 1982, the FBI created its own Hostage Rescue Team as an alternative to the military organizations and in response to perceived need for a response mechanism in the U.S.. The Posse Comitatus Act (1878) does not permit the military to be used within the U.S. without express authorization by the Constitution, through the president, or by Congress (Farrell, 1983; Gurr, 1988). In any case, the use of military forces would undoubtedly be extremely controversial and viewed only as a last resort, despite arguments in favor of facilitating the use of military antiterrorism units (see, e.g., Livingstone, 1982: 195; Tompkins, 1984; Nestlehutt, 1985).

The Department of Energy's Nuclear Emergency Search Team (NEST) also provides a response unit when nuclear materials may be involved. The U.S. Customs Service; the Bureau of Alcohol, Tobacco, and Firearms; and, the U.S. Secret Service, all within the Department of the Treasury, also have roles in preventing and responding to terrorism. The sheer number of involved agencies suggests that coordination would be a major problem and it evidently continues to be one.

What may be a critical concern, however, is whether federal

agencies will be able to respond quickly enough to distant terrorist events to provide effective counter-measures. While joint task forces and special event security preparations are used to coordinate federal, state, and local efforts in high risk locations or at high risk events (Webster, 1986), terrorists may strike almost anywhere. Local authorities often see their responsibilities as first responders largely in terms of stabilizing the situation, evaluating whether state and/or federal law enforcement agencies should be contacted, and determining whether to defer to those outside agencies when they arrive. The delay may be costly, however (Stephens, 1988).

Lastly, by presidential executive order, the Federal Emergency Management Agency had a coordinating role in the management of terrorist events. According to former FEMA director, Louis Giuffrida: " . . . FEMA is required to issue policy guidance, provide direction, and [will] control consequence management planning and implementation in . . . major incidents" (Giuffrida, 1982). Giuffrida went on to describe the FEMA role in terrorist incidents as essentially the same as its role in natural disasters and other kinds of emergencies. FEMA's role has continued to be confused, however, by a series of internal problems that resulted in the removal of several high-ranking officials in the mid-1980s (including Giuffrida), conflicts among the agency's constituent programs, and the multiplicity of government agencies sharing jurisdiction in disaster events. FEMA officials have found themselves in conflict with agencies like the NRC when they have attempted to expand FEMA's responsibilities for handling terrorist threats. The domination of FEMA by civil defense-oriented officials and the heavy-handed and highly partisan political activities of politically appointed officials in the early 1980's, moreover, lead to distrust of FEMA by state and local officials and to a lack of programmatic focus, limiting FEMA's ability to carry out its mission (see, Waugh, 1989b). While Executive Order 12656 in late 1988 reduced the role of FEMA in federal antiterrorism programs, it clarifies FEMA's coordination responsibilities and reaffirms its supporting role in the development of civil defense and national security emergency preparedness programs.

THE MODELS OF TERRORISM AND AMERICAN POLICY

As has been suggested, there are a number of ways of viewing terrorist violence and each of those models involves some basic assumptions about the nature of the violence and the appropriate responses. In brief, the six models or perceptions of terrorism noted earlier were:

1. The Revolution Model,
2. The Civil Disorder Model
3. The Law Enforcement Model,
4. The International Conflict Model,
5. The Human Rights or Repression Model, and
6. The Vigilante Model.

In terms of the models on which American policy is based, one has only to look at the structures of decisionmaking, i.e., the lead agencies and the nature of the responses. Before examining those factors, however, we can consider less focused interpretations. For example, Eric Willenz of the Carnegie Endowment for International Peace has stated that U.S. policy appears "unduly stultified by its proneness to seek a military solution for the highly differentiated and indirect threats which terrorism presents" (1987: 238). In the same article, he went on to question the American acceptance of an antiterrorism strategy of "forcible response" borrowed from the Israelis. Willenz suggested a more appropriate "multifaceted strategy" taking advantage of the U.S.'s considerable nonmilitary strengths. In short, he suggests that terrorist violence does not pose the same problems for the U.S. as it does for Israel, hence the imperative to act is somewhat different, and the options available to U.S. policymakers are much broader than they are for Israeli policymakers. The applicable models of terrorism, therefore, are fundamentally different. James Winkates draws a similar conclusion regarding the differences between U.S. and Western European responses to terrorism, suggesting that internal security measures are more common in

Western Europe because of their greater experience with internal acts of terrorism (1989). Much the same conclusion has been reached in earlier studies (e.g., Waugh, 1982, 1983, and 1989a) when the objectives of responding governments in hostage events were evidently disregarding the safety of the victims - unlike a traditional police response in which hostage safety is the primary objective. The explanation of the difference in objectives was that nations are the principal actors when terrorism is viewed from an international conflict perspective. This issue will be examined more closely after the discussion of American policy.

In terms of the American perspective on terrorism, it has been suggested that the "revolution model" is also illustrative. That model assumes a continuum of violence ranging from low level terrorism to guerrilla warfare to full-blown civil war. Military responses are appropriate to prevent an escalation of the violence and ultimately to defend the state. This is the perspective from which it has been argued that military antiterrorism forces be used. Military units were used during the turmoil of the 1960's to quell racial violence and to contain civil rights and anti-war demonstrations, as well as to force compliance with federal desegregation laws. While military personnel may have had some peripheral advisory role in responding to acts of terrorism within the U.S., legal proscription and the low level of violence has not encouraged a more active involvement.

The "civil disorder model" describes an important perception of domestic terrorist violence in the U.S. That model is based on the assumption that terrorism may be motivated by frustrated political, economic, or social interests or may possibly be less purposeful "angry violence" that can be reduced by the allevia-tion of the legitimate grievances. While it is assumed that the violence can escalate into a complete disintegration of civic order (i.e., chaos) if conditions are not ameliorated, that is generally seen as a very remote possibility. More equitable, redistributive social and economic policies are prescribed to remove the sources of frustration and anger.

By contrast, according to the "law enforcement model," terrorism is simply criminal activity, albeit with political objectives, and traditional law enforcement activities are the appropriate response. Urban policy specialists have predicted that inner cities may again see large-scale violence similar to that of the 1960s and early 1970s. They are basing their predictions on rising levels of racial violence and pointing to the increasing conflict and economic frustration due to federal cutbacks in funding for urban programs and slow state responses to urban problems. The success of urban redevelopment is not being shared with the growing urban "underclass," in other words.

The "international conflict model" is somewhat different in that individuals are not considered major actors, although they still may be considered important variables in the response equation. Such terrorism is most often viewed as a manifestation of international conflict between the U.S. and the Soviet Union or Iran or Libya (or some other identified enemy state). National security is the primary concern. National honor and prestige outweigh the other concerns.

The "repression model," like the preceding and succeeding ones, is based on a view of terrorist violence as practiced by governments or their agents against their own citizens. Law enforcement responses, as well as international sanctions, are common remedies for such violence (often defined as "state" or "official" or "repressive terrorism"). By and large, we do not see our government as being repressive, although there are coercive and repressive aspects in all governments. There is a perception among some Americans that the Reagan Administration chose not to expand federal involvement in the investigations of acts of terrorism against women's clinics because of some sympathy with the terrorists' political objectives. International human rights organizations, such as Amnesty International, have also criticized the U.S. for incidences of political repression, as well as for its use of capital punishment.

The "vigilante model" is similar, except that the issue of government support is less well defined. The violence may be explicitly or implicitly sanctioned by the government or by a significant segment of the population, e.g., an elite group. Responses to the violence are most often by law enforcement authorities or, as in the last model, by international human rights groups. Vigilante violence may be very similar to the "law enforcement model," as well, if the police are supporting or perpetrating the violence. The tolerance of and/or support for the Ku Klux Klan by some Southern law enforcement officials is a case in point. Some acts of the Posse Comitatus and The Order can also be characterized as vigilante (Gurr, 1988: 557). Gurr (1988: 559) classifies the campaign of violence against women's clinics as "vigilante terrorism," clearly fitting the FBI's definition of terrorism, despite the fact that the clinic bombings do not appear in the reports of the FBI's Terrorist Research and Analytic Center and are referred to ambiguously in Bureau of Alcohol, Tobacco, and Firearms reports.

The models only represent general perceptions, although the distinctions can be important in determining how to "manage" the violence. Certainly the dispositions of local authorities to see terrorist violence from a law enforcement perspective, the FBI to give more consideration to the political aspects of events, and the State Department to put the violence into an international conflict context will have significant impacts on how joint operations will be structured, what response options will be considered, and ultimately whether the operations are effective. For the same reasons, the coordination of joint police and military operations will also be problemmatic. Conflicts over mission and perspective, for example, will likely arise with the use of military units in federal drug interdiction operations. The use of the military in law enforcement is already controversial.

INTERVENING IN THE TERRORISM PROCESS

The model of the terrorism process developed earlier (Waugh, 1982 and 1986) follows. Added to the model are the principal means by which the U.S. government is attempting to intervene in that process to prevent and respond to terrorist violence in the U.S. and against Americans and their property overseas (Figure 1).

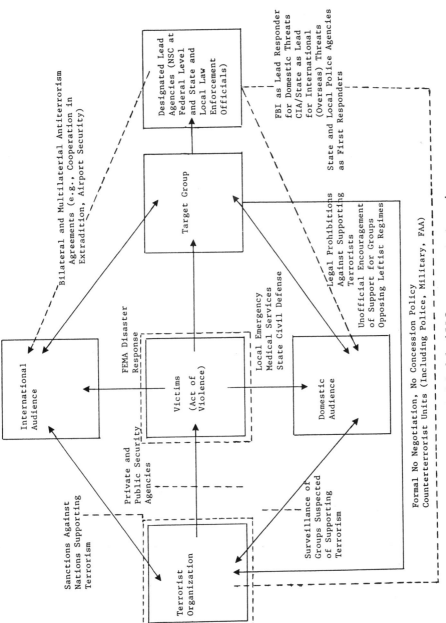

FIGURE 1. Model of U.S. response to terrorism.

The earlier analysis indicated that government interventions in the process of terrorism (using the "revolution," "civil disorder," "law enforcement," and "vigilante" models as the primary frameworks) generally will focus on:

1. Preparing for terrorism (e.g., emergency planning and preparedness),
2. Creating an environment hostile to the terrorists (e.g, forming coalitions to combat terrorists and encouraging public intolerance),
3. Alleviating precipitating conditions or creating alternative means of expressing grievances,
4. Securing likely targets,
5. Containing physical effects of terrorist attacks (e.g., clearing debris and removing casualties quickly),
6. Containing political message of terrorists,
7. Counteracting the political message of the terrorists;
8. Making the operational environment of the terrorists inhospitable (e.g., eliminating "safe houses" and inhibiting mobility),
9. Isolating terrorists from domestic and international support, and
10. Responding to specific terrorist demands.

Preparing for Terrorism

Terrorist violence is not a high salience issue in the U.S., except in the aftermath of major terrorist events. While federal offices in Washington, corporate headquarters, and airports, among other facilities, have been fortified in recent years, the level of concern has been very uneven. The organizational structures mentioned earlier attest to the importance that the federal government attaches to the threat of terrorism. That tendency to pass legislation or implement regulations in the immediate aftermath of a terrorist event and tailor it to that event, is typical of disaster responses. It is also a reason that such legislation is seldom comprehensive and seldom addresses the larger preparedness, mitigation, and response issues (May, 1985).

Security is also becoming a major issue in urban areas, in and around government and corporate facilities, and even in residential areas, although terrorism is generally less a concern than other forms of violence and criminal activity. A recent GAO study of security precautions taken around federal courts and mass transit systems points up the unevenness of preparedness activities. The GAO found that, despite some problems, the court security was relatively well developed with procedures for assessing levels of threat and evaluating security plans, but with appropriate attention to the need to keep court facilities open to the public while protecting the people involved in judicial activities. By contrast, the transit system officials appeared to assume that regular emergency response mechanisms would be able to deal with terrorism. In large measure, the transit officials did not see terrorism as a major threat (GAO, 1988b). Similarly, earlier GAO studies of nuclear powerplant security indicated that while federal licensing requirements include the development of adequate security plans, powerplants often do not integrate their plans into the other operating systems. As a result, security processes can often interfere with other emergency responses and, even, normal day-to-day operations (GAO, 1983).

Notwithstanding the unevenness of the preparation, many local governments do have special weapons and hostage negotiation teams with some capability of responding to terrorist threats. The FBI also provides training and intelligence to local authorities to increase that capability. The designation of lead agencies and other preparedness activities, however, is problemmatic in a very fragmented intergovernmental system. While federal responsibilities may be reasonably well-defined, the sheer number of local jurisdictions and less well-defined local responsibilities can create serious problems. There has been at least one case in Washington in which federal and local police have physically fought with one another over control during a hostage incident. An issue to be considered is whether the training and perspectives provided by federal authorities are appropriate for the kinds of incidents that local police agencies may face. To the extent that violence may be used in response to state or local policies, the federal approach may be inappropriate.

Local resources for antiterrorism activities are very limited. Cities like New York have considerable experience with hostage events and bombings, indeed often more experience than federal authorities, and capacities to respond to terrorist events are quite good. Those well-equipped localities are the exception rather than the rule, however.

Creating Hostile Environment for Terrorists

The most common means of creating a hostile environment for terrorists to inhibit their operations is the development of legal vehicles for the apprehension and prosecution of terrorists. The American legal system continues to develop such vehicles. Most of the acts of violence that may be perpetrated by terrorists are covered by United States criminal law. The larger issue is whether state and local law enforcement agencies will have jurisdiction over incidences of terrorist violence rather than federal agencies. By and large, that is in fact the case unless the nature of the facilities (e.g., airport, nuclear plant, or military installation) or persons (e.g., federal officials) attacked, the weapon (e.g., bomb), or the act (e.g., kidnapping or bank robbery) gives federal agencies jurisdiction.

One of the most common types of terrorist violence in the United States has been directed against civilian aviation, airports and/or aircraft. The United States is a signatory of the Tokyo Convention of 1963 (Convention on Offenses and Certain Other Acts Committed on Board Aircraft), the Hague Convention of 1970 (Convention for the Suppression of Unlawful Seizure of Aircraft), and the Montreal Convention of 1971 (Convention for the Suppression of Unlawful Acts Against the Safety of Civil Aviation). Those three conventions clarify jurisdiction in incidents involving international aviation and encourage signatories and others to prosecute persons who interfere with civil aviation or to extradite them to a nation that will prosecute them. Similarly, other multilateral agreements and conventions have clarified the roles of nations involved directly or indirectly in international terrorist events. The U.S.-Cuban anti-hijacking treaty is a case in point in terms of its effectiveness in reducing the number of aerial hijackings to Havana.

The Anti-Hijacking Act of 1974 (P.L. 93-366) was enacted to bring the Federal Aviation Act of 1958 into conformity with the Hague Convention (US Department of State, 1979; GAO, 1987b, 1988d). Subsequent amendments to the 1958 Act have developed and expanded the Air Carrier Standard Security Program, which requires air carriers to provide security for aircraft and facilities, including screening of passengers and luggage before boarding. Following the 1985 hijacking of a TWA flight in Athens, Greece, and a lengthy spectacle in Beirut (see: Waugh and Sweeney, 1988), Congress enacted the International Security and Development Cooperation Act (P.L. 99-83) which increased Federal Aviation Administration monitoring of security at foreign airports serving American carriers and foreign carriers flying to the U.S.

The Secretary of Transportation is responsible for publicizing the identities of airports that fail to provide adequate security. If conditions are not improved, the Secretary of State can issue travel advisories warning the public and, ultimately, the president can prohibit U.S. and other airlines serving the U.S. from using that airport (GAO, 1988d). Security at the Athens, Greece, airport was questioned in 1985 following the TWA hijacking.

The Department of Transportation is stepping up its efforts to develop effective security devices. For example, Thermal Neutron Analysis technologies are being developed to provide a better means of identifying plastic explosives, such as those used in the Pan Am Flight 103 bombing in 1988. Two such devices were displayed at the Paris Air Show in June of 1989 at the invitation of the FAA. Representatives of seven Western democracies met in January of 1989 to discuss the threat of plastic explosives and have raised the possibility of an international convention requiring the "tagging" of plastic explosives during their manufacture with substances that can be detected using current technologies. That option is being pursued now. The interagency counterterrorism R&D program, under the leadership of State Department officials, is also pursuing other options (McManaway, 1989).

The U.S. Department of State, through its Anti-Terrorism Training Assistance (ATA) Program, also has been training foreign nationals involved in aviation and other areas of security and providing funding for security equipment. The ATA program was established in 1983 and, as well as facilitating the protection of Americans overseas, provides a vehicle for interaction among American and foreign antiterrorism specialists and strengthens the foreign governments' capacities to protect themselves. The program includes policy discussions with and briefings of high-level foreign officials in the U.S., the design of an appropriate assistance program with the help of a U.S. team sent to that nation, and a training program conducted in the U.S. The training programs include such topics as airport police management, maritime security, and bomb disposal (McManaway, 1987).

The U.S. government is prohibited from providing military training to foreign police, because of the involvement of U.S.-trained security troops in Latin America in the torture and murder of dissidents during the 1960s and early 1970s. Nonetheless, it was reported in the *Los Angeles Times* in 1989 that the U.S. military, the FAA, the CIA, the FBI, and the State Department are all involved in training and providing technical assistance to foreign counterterrorism units. The report went on to say that American counterterrorism unit members have been directly involved in foreign counterterrorism operations, such as the rescue of hostages held by rebels in the Sudan in July of 1983 (including two Americans) and the storming of a hijacked Venezuelan plane in Curacao in July of 1984 (*Atlanta Constitution*, July 3, 1989).

The U.S. is also party to the U.N.'s 1973 Convention on the Prevention and Punishment of Crimes Against Internationally Protected Persons (General Assembly Resolution 3166). P.L. 92-539 in 1972, predating the convention, amended U.S. law to provide protection for foreign officials and guests of the U.S. government. Special protection of diplomatic agents was further expanded by P.L. 94-467 in 1976, which implemented the U.N. Convention, gave jurisdiction over offenses to U.S. federal courts, and opened the way for the Attorney General to seek military assistance in enforcing the law (Department of State, 1979).

To illustrate the application of American law in response to international terrorism, the following are the most relevent statutes (GAO, 1987c):

Export Administration Act of 1979 (P.L. 96-72) and 1985 Amendments (P.L. 99-64)

International Emergency Economic Powers Act of 1977 (P.L. 95-223)

Federal Aviation Act of 1958 (P.L. 85-726) and 1985 Amendments (P.L. 99-83)

National Emergencies Act of 1976 (P.L. 94-412)

International Security and Development Cooperation Act of 1985 (P.L. 99-83)

Arms Export Control Act of 1968 (P.L. 90-629) and 1986 Amendments (P.L. 99-399)

Export-Import Bank Act of 1945

Foreign Assistance Act of 1961 (P.L. 87-195) and amendments

Trade Expansion Act of 1962 (P.L. 87-794)

Immigration and Nationality Act of 1952

Omnibus Diplomatic Security and Antiterrorism Act of 1986 (P.L. 99-399)

Trade Act of 1974 (P.L. 93-618) and amendments

Trading with the Enemy Act of 1917 and 1977 Amendment (P.L. 95-223)

The Export Adminstration Act of 1979 has been most used, largely to restrict trade between the U.S. and Libya, Syria, Iraq, Cuba, Iran, and the People's Democratic Republic of Yemen. All six of those nations have been identified at one time or another as supporting terrorist activity. The Act has been used to deny export licenses for aircraft, aircraft parts, turbine engine cores for ships, off-highway vehicles, and other items that might have military uses (GAO, 1987c).

The other statutes have been similarly used against those same six nations. The International Emergency Economic Powers Act has been used to prevent the return of Iranian assets in the U.S. and to restrict other transactions with Iran and Libya. The International Security and Development Cooperation Act of 1985 has been used to ban imports from Libya. The Federal Aviation Act has been used to ban the sale of airline tickets in the U.S. for travel which includes stops in Libya and tickets for Syrian Arab Airlines (GAO, 1987c). The bans on travel have not always been entirely successful, such as those on travel to Cuba and Iran, but the potential to limit interaction is certainly there.

The objective here is not to provide a complete overview of applicable international law, but it is important to note that the principle of *aut dedere aut judicare*, that nations should prosecute terrorists or extradite them to a nation that will, still does not find universal support. The U.S. has been a major proponent of that principle. However, many nations, particularly in Latin American and northern Europe, have long histories of granting asylum to persons fleeing prosecution for political crimes and those nations understandably resist efforts to apply antiterrorism laws too broadly. In short, American efforts to develop international consensus on broad definitions of terrorism and terrorists have not been successful. More success has been achieved in banning specific categories of violence, such as attacks on diplomatic personnel and facilities and on aircraft. Those successes should not be overstated, however. Given the nature of international law and the realities of international politics, it is much easier to claim legal jurisdiction than it is to act upon it.

The Doherty case raises other important issues concerning American policy and the effectiveness of international cooperation. Joe Doherty was convicted in British courts for participating in a 1980 Irish Republican Army attack that resulted in the death of a British army officer. He escaped from prison in Northern Ireland in 1981 and was apprehended by Federal Bureau of Investigation agents in a suburb of New York City in June of 1983. Doherty's lawyers contend that his crime was politically motivated and thus qualify him for political asylum in the U.S. The federal district court judge who heard the case brought by the British government, the district judge who heard the case brought by the U.S. government, and the U.S. Court of Appeals panel who heard the U.S. government's appeal all ruled in favor of Doherty. The U.S. Justice Department's attempts to have Doherty deported to Britain were frustrated when the immigration judge ruled that Doherty could elect to be deported to the Republic of Ireland. The U.S./British extradition treaty that excluded extradition for politically motivated acts was renegotiated in 1986 and the exclusion clause was dropped (*Atlanta Journal and Constitution*, November 24, 1988). Notwithstanding the fact that both the U.S. and British governments were strongly in favor of extradition, the Doherty case does illustrate the problems involved in implementing policies based on the principle of *aut dedere aut judicare*. The proposed "Terrorist Alien Removal Act," if passed by Congress, would facilitate extradition of known and suspected terrorists (presumably like Doherty) from the U.S. (Bremer, 1988).

The greatest potential for using law to fight terrorism is perhaps in the application of American law enforcement procedures. In 1984, laws were passed to outlaw the taking of Americans hostage overseas. In 1986, assaulting, maiming, or murdering U.S. citizens overseas became illegal under U.S. criminal law. That approach was tested in 1987 when the FBI arrested a Lebanese terrorist in 1987, by luring him to a boat in international waters off the coast of Cyprus (Martin and Walcott, 1988). The policy was the product of a national security finding in 1986 that authorized the CIA to identify terrorists known to have committed crimes against American citizens and to assist in their apprehension so that they could be brought to the U.S. for trial. The capture of the terrorist, Fawaz Younis, who was involved in the TWA hijacking in 1985, was a joint operation involving the FBI, the U.S. Navy (a pilot from the U.S.S. Saratoga flew Younis directly to the U.S. from the Mediterranean), the CIA, and the Drug Enforcement Agency. Despite having taped evidence in which Younis confessed to participating the the 1985 hijacking and a signed confession given after capture, there are still questions concerning the legality of the evidence given by a prisoner unfamiliar with U.S. law and being held in a cramped and hot cabin on the vessel (Emerson, 1988). The expansion of law enforcement programs designed for drug interdiction and the apprehension of those involved in the international drug trade, such as programs to pay large cash rewards for information and programs for witness protection, may also provide legal foundation for antiterrorism programs.

National Security Directive 138, signed by President Reagan on April 3, 1984, called upon twenty-six federal agencies to provide options to the administration, permitted the expansion of intelligence gathering efforts, and stepped up the development of antiterrorism forces. Potential targets were identified, contingency plans were developed, and sensitive facilities were "hardened."

Less encouraging have been the 1985 Reagan Administration decision permitting the kidnapping of suspected terrorists and the suggestions that counterterrorist forces might be used to assassinate suspected terrorists.

It must also be noted that many analysts point out that the restrictions placed on American intelligence agencies, as well as budgetary cutbacks, following the excesses of the 1960s and early 1970s have made it extremely difficult to gather needed information on terrorist activities (see, e.g., Jenkins, 1977; Horchem, 1981; Tompkins, 1984; Nestlehutt, 1985; and, Martin and Walcott, 1988). Congressional support for increased intelligence-gathering capacities may be one of the victims of the Iran-Contra affair. Currently, Congress is showing less willingness to spend scarce tax dollars on more national security programs and perhaps some distrust of the national security apparatus. At the same time, officials involved in the antiterrorism program are calling for increased covert activity to infiltrate, surveil, and subvert terrorist organizations (see, e.g., Bremer, 1988).

Alleviation of Precipitating Conditions

The official responses to terrorist violence seldom focus on the alleviation of precipitating conditions. Indeed, there seems to have been a very conscious avoidance by American officials of any suggestion that terrorist violence may be justified. Having said that, it must also be noted that the American government has expressed concerns recently about violence practiced by governments against their own citizens or other residents, more specifically the violence used by Israel against Palestinian protesters during the "Intifada," or by vigilante groups, such as the "death squads" supported by the more conservative elements in El Salvador. The ambiguous nature of terrorist violence makes it easier to term friendly terrorists "freedom fighters" than it is to attempt to justify terrorism more directly. The American foreign policy establishment, following the collapse of the regimes of the Shah in Iran and Ferdinand Marcos in the Philippines, does appear to be more aware of the importance of the popular underpinnings of governments and more willing to suggest creating forums for political dissent.

Providing Security

While it is impossible to identify, let alone secure, all possible terrorist targets, some success has been achieved in reducing the number of attacks. The most obvious case is airport facilities. The frequency of armed attacks and bombings of airports, as well as aerial hijackings, has certainly declined since the peak years of violence in the late 1960s and early 1970s. However, 1986 assessments of airport security in the U.S. by the FAA have demonstrated that approximately 20% of the weapons taken through current security devices are not detected. The security systems tested were in "category X" or the highest risk airports.

As a result of those and subsequent FAA tests, the practice of allowing airline personnel to bypass the security checks was stopped and checks on other airline and airport personnel were stepped up.

Following the disintegration of Pan Am Flight 103 over Lockerbie, Scotland, in December of 1988, the debate concerning the official U.S. government role in warning passengers of credible threats to aviation heated up. In response to criticism of the FAA, largely due to the failure to warn civilian travelers of the threat despite warnings provided to State Department and other U.S. personnel, the Department of Transportation announced in April of 1989 that American air carriers will be required to acknowledge all FAA security bulletins within twenty-four hours. The Secretary of Transportation, Samuel K. Skinner, also announced that air carriers are required to install security devices capable of detecting plastic explosives like those that destroyed Flight 103. Further proposals included the installation of state-of-the-art detection equipment and providing "appropriate security information" to pilots (*Atlanta Journal and Constitution*, April 4, 1989). The issue of whether to notify travelers of all terrorist threats or to continue judging the credibility of threats before making them public is still unresolved, although the FAA is providing more guidance to air carriers. The responsibility for providing warning of credible threats may be defined somewhat better in one or more of the lawsuits stemming from the Flight 103 bombing.

Currently, businesses can get information on the risk to their personnel in locations overseas through the State Department's Overseas Security Advisory Council by computer link and other travelers can get advisories by telephone through the Citizens Emergency Center. But, neither system provides information on specific threats to aviation.

Containing Physical Destruction (The Threat)

The development of emergency medical services capabilities specifically for terrorist events is still not a common practice in the

U.S. By and large, most localities assume either that normal emergency procedures will be adequate in the event of terrorist violence or that the risk is so ill-defined that more focused procedures cannot be reasonably designed and implemented. In other words, terrorism can take so many forms and its intensity can vary so greatly that there is no assurrance that preparations will be appropriate. The Federal Emergency Management Agency's capacity to respond to disastrous events of all types may provide much more elasticity, particularly if the U.S. experiences high casualty and/or high destruction terrorism (Waugh, 1986).

Containing Political Message and Counteracting Terrorist Propaganda

The U.S. government, as well as the governments of other democratic societies, is inhibited in its ability to "contain" the political message of terrorists. There have been suggestions that authorities and the media simply report events without crediting specific terrorist organizations for the violence, but such suggestions have not found widespread support among journalists or public officials. Democratic societies may in fact have some advantage in counteracting terrorist propaganda. To the extent that the media report accurate information and provide adequate analysis for the public to interpret events, open media coverage should be beneficial. However, an active and open media generally will limit the ability of government officials to contain and structure the communication concerning a terrorist event. The success of the Reagan Administration in maintaining secrecy prior to and controlling information during the military operation in Grenada, for example, resulted in the media seeking information from authorities in Havana. Indeed, according to media spokespersons at the time, the information forthcoming from Havana was more complete and accurate than that provided by U.S. military authorities.

The attention recent presidents have given to the problem of terrorism give it salience as issue, but may well have increased the impact of the violence. To the extent that terrorists seek publicity, commanding the attention of the chief executive magnifies the effect of the violent acts (Waugh, 1983). The fact that such events frequently dominate the news and often are the principal topics in presidential press conferences makes them seem much more important than their costs would suggest. However, if the public and the media do expect direct presidential involvement in the resolution of terrorist incidents, the events may be important measures of presidential effectiveness. Certainly, the Iran hostage crisis had a profound impact on the presidential election of 1980.

Increasing Police Pressure

The FBI and other law enforcement agencies have been remarkably effective in monitoring potentially violent organizations, intervening to stop terrorist operations, and apprehending terrorists. In 1985, for example, the FBI prevented violence by and/or arrested members of the New Afrikan Freedom Fighters; United Freedom Front; May 19th Communist Organization; The Covenant, the Sword, and Arm of the Lord; "The Order;" Sikh extremists; and, pro-Libyan groups, as well as others. International terrorist groups, with a few exceptions such as Croatian and Armenian nationalists, have had little success operating in the U.S. (FBI, 1988).

Isolating of Terrorists from Support

The combination of increased border security, international antiterrorism agreements (including exchanges of information), specific legislation proscribing economic and political ties to identified "terrorist nations," efforts to interdict shipments of weapons and other terrorist materiel across national borders, surveillance of suspected terrorists and possible supporters, and other activities have acted to isolate terrorists from possible international support. Monitoring of domestic groups has been somewhat more problemmatic, particularly given concerns about abuses of police power during the 1960's and early 1970's. Information is shared by federal and local authorities, however.

Responding to Specific Terrorist Demands

By and large, the objective of American law enforcement agencies in hostage cases has been to negotiate releases within certain bounds. In short, police policies frequently set parameters for negotiation, i.e., particular kinds of concessions that would not be made under any circumstances. The development of the Bolz-Schlossberg technique by the New York City hostage negotiation team, including its more recent permutations and related techniques, and its adoption by other law enforcement agencies has become an effective response in barricade and hostage cases. Indeed, it is so effective that there have been indications that terrorists have studied the technique to reduce their vulnerability to manipulation by negotiators. Other kinds of demands may be addressed by state and local authorities on a case-by-case basis, although there are likely to be very strong pressures to adopt the national policy. However, it is doubtful that state and local political leaders can show the same firmness in the face potential hostage casualties as can a president. Certainly a law enforcement perspective would not support such firmness. Local officials will find it easiest to treat terrorist events as one would any other kind of criminal activity, albeit a very serious one, or to let state or federal authorities assume jurisdiction and responsibility for losses.

   The official policy of the U.S. regarding terrorist demands is to offer no concessions. The origins of that policy are generally traced to statements by President Nixon in 1970 when the Saudi Arabian embassy in Khartoum, Sudan, was seized by members of the Black September Organization. Soon after the initial statement, the two American diplomats and the Belgian charge d'affairs were killed. The logic of the policy is that concessions will only lead to more violence (Farrell, 1983). That logic was spelled out by Henry Kissinger in an August 1975 speech after the U.S. ambassador to

Tanzania, W. Beverly Carter, facilitated the payment of ransom for two American students (*National Review*, 1975). Kissinger said that:

> The problem that arises in the case of terrorist attacks on Americans has to be seen not only in relation to the individual case but in relation to the thousands of Americans who are in jeopardy all over the world. In every individual case, the overwhelming temptation is to go along with what is being asked.
>
> On the other hand, if terrorist groups get the impression that they can force a negotiation with the United States and an acquiescence in their demands, then we may save lives in one place at the risk of hundreds of lives everywhere else.
>
> Therefore it is our policy . . . that American Ambassadors and American officials not participate in negotiations on the release of victims of terrorists and that terrorists know that the United States will not participate in the payment of ransom and in the negotiation for it (1978).

The veracity of that position has been called into question recently because of the Reagan Administration's attempts in the mid-1980's to trade arms to Iran in exchange for American hostages held in Lebanon. There have been earlier indications, albeit more rumors than documented cases, that other Administrations have ransomed American hostages in the Middle East.

CONCLUSIONS: THE EMERGENCY MANAGEMENT MODEL AND AMERICAN POLICY

The examination of American antiterrorism policy is of necessity somewhat superficial. It is difficult to get a real feel for the adequacy and effectiveness of policies and programs without testing under a variety of realistic conditions. FEMA, the FBI, and FAA, among other agencies, are testing preparedness and mitigation programs, but the results of those tests are not generally made public. The GAO findings suggest that some holes do exist in current programs.

Nonetheless, the description of antiterrorism policies and programs provided here do permit some examination of current policy. In brief, the national policy is one based on three elements: (1) not acceding to terrorist demands, (2) identifying and punishing states that support terrorism, and (3) using the "force of law" to apprehend, try, and punish terrorists (Bremer, 1988). The tenor of that policy currently is proactive, emphasizing the need for offensive "counterterrorism" programs rather than more defensive "antiterrorism" efforts. The question is how the American response to terrorism fits the emergency management model (or how the response can be made to fit the model).

In large measure, the interventions in the terrorism process clearly indicate that American policy addresses the need for preparedness. However, some agencies exhibit very high levels of preparedness and others very low levels. The highest risk areas have generally been identified, although many have not been secured. The great number of potential targets suggests that providing security would be prohibitively expensive. That is undoubtedly the reasoning behind the current emphasis on counterterrorism programs.

At the federal level, the areas that have been identified as high risk do appear to have operational plans with lead agencies, cooperative agreements, mechanisms for liaison and coordination, communications networks, public information channels, and training and education programs. The "Assignment of Emergency Preparedness Responsibilities" in EO 12656 do provide some guidelines for national security emergency preparedness policy and identify many of the major areas of concern. However, as was apparent in the analysis of the risk to maritime facilities in the U.S., there are some serious gaps in that preparation. It is also uncertain whether resource management capabilities have been developed for non-civil defense types of emergency. The FEMA disaster response mechanisms for providing shelter, emergency food, mass evacuations, and other support services presumably would be put into operation during a major mass destruction terrorist event. If necessary, a presidential disaster declaration would make the affected locality eligible for additional federal support and services (see, e.g., Settle, 1989). As outlined in EO 12656, in national security-related disasters, additional resources would be provided by: the Departments of Agriculture, Commerce, Defense, Education, Energy, Health and Human Services, Housing and Urban Development, the Interior, Justice, Labor, State, Transportation, and the Treasury; the Environmental Protection Agency; the General Services Administration; the National Aeronautics and Space Administration; National Archives and Records Administration; Nuclear Regulatory Commission; Office of Personnel Management; Selective Service System; Tennessee Valley Authority; U.S. Information Agency; U.S. Postal Service; Veterans Administration; and, the Office of Management and Budget.

Similarly, programs to mitigate the effects of terrorism also appear to be in place. Law enforcement and intelligence agencies are acting to assure that major terrorist campaigns and mass destruction acts are difficult to implement. The relatively small number of terrorist events attests to the effectiveness of such mitigation efforts. The attention that the GAO has paid to the FAA's monitoring of airports and the NRC's monitoring of nuclear plant security also supports the conclusion that the vulnerability of potential targets is being assessed periodically.

The FBI is providing technical assistance and training to state and local agencies, as well as other federal agencies. The FAA and the Department of State are providing technical assistance and training to foreign nationals, as well as to U.S. security offices. Borders are being watched, and so on. The continued availability of military-type automatic weapons in the U.S. remains a significant problem, however. Terrorist and criminal organizations have ready access to some of the most advanced military weaponry. Mitigation efforts have also kept within the bounds of American law, i.e., civil liberties have not been abridged to facilitate security, although there have been suggestions that police powers be increased.

International treaties, particularly involving cooperative efforts with other governments combatting terrorism, reduce the likelihood of major incidences of violence. There are even some indications that the current Administration is attempting to reduce the likelihood of violence by alleviating precipitative conditions. The concern shown for the popular underpinnings of the new government in El Salvador and its economic policies is a case in point.

The effectiveness of American response programs is difficult to measure given the few publicized cases. The question of whether local agencies can respond adequately to terrorist events is difficult to answer. In recent cases involving right-wing terrorist groups, the FBI have been called in to assist local law enforcement agencies (FBI, 1988). The failed Iran hostage rescue raised fundamental issues about the capacity of the military special operations units to respond to terrorist events abroad. It is unclear whether the subsequent investigations have resulted in adequate measures to prevent similiar failures (Waugh, 1987).

The assumption is that the resources of FEMA will be mobilized if needed in a terrorism-related disaster response. Similarly, it is assumed that FEMA will be involved in any necessary recovery efforts in support of state and local emergency management agencies and nonprofit disaster relief agencies as it would in any other emergency.

The relatively new emphasis on law enforcement responses to international, as well as domestic, terrorism does suggest that there is a fundamental change in policy underway. The relative success of American law enforcement agencies in responding to domestic terrorism may carry over to the international arena, particularly in dealing with transnational terrorist organizations. The implicit adoption of the "law enforcement" model may also mean that some of the assumptions concerning the nature of the violence are also changing. The organizational context of American policy is an important indicator of the range of solutions under consideration and the nature of the policy objectives.

REFERENCES

Yonah Alexander, David Carlton, and Paul Wilkinson, eds. *Terrorism: Theory and Practice* (Boulder, Colo.: Westview Press, 1979).

Atlanta Journal and Constitution (1989) "Sky-High Security: U.S. Shapes Strategy as Mourners Lobby," April 4, p. 3A.

Atlanta Journal and Constitution (1988) "IRA Member in U.S. Custody Is Called Hero, Terrorist," November 24, p. 92A.

Atlanta Journal and Constitution (1989) "Americans Must Die, Iran Official Proclaims," May 6, pp. 1A and 8A.

Atlanta Journal and Constitution (1989) "U.S. 'Rambos' Skip Red Tape, Secretly Train Foreign Squads," July 3, p. 2A.

Dudley Barker (1959) *Grivas: Portrait of a Terrorist* (New York: Harcourt, Brace and Company).

J. Bowyer Bell (1978) *A Time of Terror: How Democratic Societies Respond to Revolutionary Violence* (New York: Basic Books, 1978).

Robert G. Bell (1976) "The U.S. Response to Terrorism Against International Civil Aviation," *Orbis* 19 (Winter): 1326-1343.

Warren A. Bradish (1986) "The Worldwide Terrorist Threat and the U.S. Counter Strategy," Presentation for Panel on "Terrorism and the Businessman," Georgia State University, Atlanta, October 24.

L. Paul Bremer, III (1987) "Counterterrorism: Strategy and Tactics" (Reprint of Speech before the Committee on Foreign Relations, Tampa, Florida, November 4, 1987). Washington, DC: US Department of State, Bureau of Public Affairs, Current Policy No. 1023, November.

L. Paul Bremer, III (1988) "Countering Terrorism in the 1980s and 1990s" (Reprint of Address before the George Washington University conference on Terrorism, Washington, DC, November 22, 1987). Washington, DC: US Department of State, Bureau of Public Affairs, December.

Richard D. Crabtree, LTC (1985) "High Technology Terrorism: Responding to Nuclear, Chemical, and Biological Attack," Paper presented at the Workshop on Emergency Management, National Conference of the American Society for Public Administration, Indianapolis, Indiana, April.

Ronald D. Crelinsten, Danielle Laberge-Altmejd, and Denis Szabo (1978) *Terrorism and Criminal Justice: An International Perspective* (Lexington, Mass.: Lexington Books).

Brian Crozier (1960) *The Rebels: A Study of Post-War Insurrections* (Boston:

Beacon Press).

Yehezkel Dror (1983) "Terrorism as a Challenge to the Democratic Capacity to Govern," pp. 65-90 in *Terrorism, Legitimacy, and Power*, edited by Martha Crenshaw (Middletown, Conn.: Wesleyan University Press).

John D. Elliot and Leslie K. Gibson, eds. (1978) *Contemporary Terrorism* (Gaithersburg, Md.: International Association of Chiefs of Police).

Steven Emerson (with Richard Rothschild) (1988) "Taking on Terrorists," *U.S. News and World Report* (September 12), pp. 26-34.

Alona E. Evans and John F. Murphy, eds. (1978) *Legal Aspects of International Terrorism* (Lexington, Mass.: Lexington Books).

Ernest Evans (1979) *Calling a Truce to Terror: The American Response to International Terrorism* (Westport, Conn.: Greenwood Press).

Robert A. Fearey (1978) "Introduction to International Terrorism," in *International Terrorism in the Contemporary World*, edited by Marius H. Livingston (Westport, Conn.: Greenwood Press).

William Regis Farrell (1982) *The U.S. Government Response to Terrorism: In Search of an Effective Strategy* (Boulder, Colo.: Westview Press).

Federal Bureau of Investigation (1988) "Terrorism at Home and Abroad: The U.S. Government View," pp. 295-372 in *The Politics of Terrorism*, Third Edition, edited by Michael Stohl (New York: Marcel Dekker).

Louis O. Giuffrida (1982a) "FEMA and Consequences of Terrorism," *Law Enforcement Communication* (December), p. 15.

Louis O. Giuffrida (1982b) "Acts of Terrorism: How is FEMA Responding?," *Hazard Monthly* (December), p. 1.

Ted Robert Gurr (1988) "Political Terrorism in the United States: Historical Antecedents and Contemporary Trends," pp. 549-578 in *The Politics of Terrorism*, Third Edition, edited by Michael Stohl (New York: Marcel Dekker).

Martin F. Herz (1982) *Diplomats and Terrorists: What Works, What Doesn't - A Symposium* (Washington, DC: Georgetown University, Institute for the Study of Diplomacy).

Hans Josef Horchem (1981) "Pre-Empting Terror," in *International Terrorism*, edited by Benjamin Netanyahu (Jerusalem: The Jonathan Institute).

Brian Michael Jenkins (1971) *The Five Stages of Guerrilla Warfare: Challenge of the 1970s*, Santa Monica, Calif.: Rand Corporation, P-4670, July.

Brian Michael Jenkins (1975) *High Technology Terrorism and Surrogate War: The Impact of New Technology on Low-Level Violence*, Santa Monica, Calif.: Rand Corporation, P-5339.

Brian Michael Jenkins (1975) *International Terrorism: A New Mode of Conflict* (Los Angeles: Crescent Publications).

Brian Michael Jenkins (1977) *Combatting International Terrorism: The Role of Congress*, Santa Monica, Calif.: Rand Corporation, P-5808, January.

Brian Michael Jenkins (1979) *The Consequences of Nuclear Terrorism*, Santa Monica, Calif.: Rand Corporation, P-6373, August.

Brian Michael Jenkins (1984) *Combatting International Terrorism Becomes a War*, Santa Monica, Calif.: Rand Corporation, P-6988, May.

Robert Kupperman and Darrell Trent (1979) *Terrorism: Threat, Reality, Response* (Stanford, Calif.: Hoover Institution Press).

Neil C. Livingstone (1982) *The War Against Terrorism* (Lexington, Mass.: Lexington Books).

Clayton E. McManaway, Jr. (1987) "Testimony on the Anti-Terrorism Training Assistance Program, Fiscal Year 1988, presented to the U.S. House of Representatives, Appropriations Subcommittee on Foreign Operations, April 22." Washington, DC: Department of State.

Clayton E. McManaway, Jr. (1989) "Testimony of Ambassador Clayton E. McManaway, Jr., Associate Coordinator, Office of the Ambassador-at-Large for Counterterrorism, Department of State, to the Subcommittee on Aviation of the Commerce Committee, U.S. Senate, April 13." Washington, DC: Department of State.

David C. Martin and John Walcott, *Best Laid Plans: The Inside Story of America's War Against Terrorism* (New York: Harper and Row, 1988).

David L. Milbank (1976) *International and Transnational Terrorism: Diagnosis and Prognosis*, Washington, DC: US Central Intelligence Agency, PR-10030, April.

Eric Morris and Alan Hoe (1988) *Terrorism: Threat and Response* (New York: St. Martin's Press).

National Review (1975) "How Not to Combat Terrorism," 12 September.

M.S. Nestlehutt (1985) "Combating Terrorism," Atlanta, Georgia: Georgia State University, unpublished paper.

James M. Poland (1988) *Understanding Terrorism: Groups, Strategies, and Responses* (New York: Prentice-Hall).

Anthony C.E. Quainton (1978) "Government Policy and Response in a Terrorist Crisis Situation" (Address before the Chicago Association of Commerce and Industry, September 26),Washington, DC: U.S. Department of State, mimeographed.

Anthony C.E. Quainton (1983) "Terrorism and Political Violence: A Permanent Challenge to Governments," pp. 52-64 in *Terrorism, Legitimacy, and Power*, edited by Martha Crenshaw (Middletown,

Conn.: Wesleyan University Press).

Linda K. Richter and William L. Waugh, Jr. (1986) "Terrorism and Tourism as Logical Companions," *Tourism Management* (December): 230-238.

Richard H. Schultz, Jr., and Stephen Sloan, eds. (1981) *Responding to the Terrorist Threat: Security and Crisis Management* (Elmsford, N.Y.: Pergamon Press).

Allen K. Settle (1989) "Disaster Assistance: Securing Presidential Declarations," in *Cities and Disaster: North American Studies in Emergency Management*, edited by Richard T. Sylves and William L. Waugh, Jr. (Springfield, Ill.: Charles C. Thomas Publishers).

J.D. Simon (1987) *Misperceiving the Terrorist Threat*, Santa Monica, Calif.: The Rand Corporation, Rand Report R-3423-RC, June.

Col. Charles M. Simpson (1984) "'Paranoia' as Weapon in Unconventional Warfare," *Army* (April), pp. 30-33.

Stephen Sloan (1981) *Simulating Terrorism* (Norman, Okla.: University of Oklahoma Press).

Hugh W. Stephens (1988) "Agency Jurisdiction and the Defense of Maritime Facilities in the United States," Paper delivered at the Annual Meeting of the International Studies Association-South, Atlanta, Georgia, November 4.

Richard T. Sylves and Thomas J. Pavlak (1989) "The Big Apple and Disaster Planning: How New York City Manages Major Emergencies," in *Cities and Disaster: North American Studies in Emergency Management*, edited by Richard T. Sylves and William L. Waugh, Jr. (Springfield, Ill.: Charles C. Thomas Publishers).

Thomas C. Tompkins (1984) *Military Countermeasures to Terrorism in the 1980s*, Santa Monica, Calif.: Rand Corporation, N-2178-RC, August.

Darrell M. Trent (1979) "A National Policy to Combat Terrorism," *Policy Review* 9 (Summer): 41-53.

U.S. Army (1978) *The USAICS Handbook on Urban Terrorism*, Fort Huachuca, Ariz.: US Army Intelligence Center and School, SupR 03317-1, June.

U.S. Central Intelligence Agency (n.d.) *Intelligence: The Acme of Skill*, Washington, DC: CIA.

U.S. Department of Justice (1977) *Facing Tomorrow's Terrorist Incident Today*, Washington, DC: Department of Justice, October.

U.S. Department of State (1979) "Terrorism: Summary of Applicable United States and International Law," (Memographed Report, n.d.).

U.S. Department of State (1986) *Patterns of Global Terrorism: 1985*,

Washington, DC: Department of State, October. Reprinted in *The Politics of Terrorism*, 3rd edition, edited by Michael Stohl (New York and Basel: Marcel Dekker, 1988)

U.S. Department of State (1989) *Patterns of Global Terrorism: 1988*, Washington, DC: Department of State, March.

U.S. General Accounting Office (1977) *F.B.I. Domestic Intelligence Operations: An Uncertain Future*, Washington, DC: USGAO, GGD-78-237, December 21.

U.S. General Accounting Office (1983) *Additional Improvements Needed in Physical Security at Nuclear Powerplants*, Washington, DC: USGAO, GAO/RCED-83-141, July 13.

U.S. General Accounting Office (1984) *Status of the Department of State's Security Enhancement Program*, Washington, DC: USGAO, GAO/NSIAD-84-163, September 14.

U.S. General Accounting Office (1986) *Embassy Security: State Department's Efforts to Improve Security Overseas*, Washington, DC: USGAO, GAO/NSIAD-86-133, June 12.

U.S. General Accounting Office (1987a) *Terrorism: Laws Cited Imposing Sanctions on Nations Supporting Terrorism*, Washington, DC: USGAO, GAO/RCED-87-133FS, April 17.

U.S. General Accounting Office (1987b) *Aviation Security: FAA Preboard Passenger Screening Test Results*, Washington, DC: USGAO, GAO/RECD-87-125FS, April 30.

U.S. General Accounting Office (1988a) *Aviation Security: Improved Controls Needed to Prevent Unauthorized Access at Key Airports*, Washington, DC: USGAO, GAO/RCED-88-86, January 29.

U.S. General Accounting Office (1988b) *Domestic Terrorism: Prevention Efforts in Selected Federal Courts and Mass Transit Systems*, Washington, DC: USGAO, GAO/PEMD-88-22, June 23.

U.S. General Accounting Office (1988c) *Nuclear Security: DOE Actions to Improve the Personnel Clearance Program*, Washington, DC: USGAO, GAO/RCED-89-34, November 9.

U.S. General Accounting Office (1988d) *Aviation Security: FAA's Assessments of Foreign Airports*, Washington, DC: USGAO, GAO/RCED-89-45, December 7.

William L. Waugh, Jr. (1982) *International Terrorism: How Nations Respond to Terrorists* (Chapel Hill, N.C.: Documentary Publications).

William L. Waugh, Jr. (1983) "The Values in Violence: Organizational and Political Objectives of Terrorist Groups," *Conflict Quarterly* (Summer): 1-19.

William L. Waugh, Jr. (1986) "Integrating the Policy Models of Terrorism and Emergency Management," *Policy Studies Review* (Fall): 287-300.

William L. Waugh, Jr. (1987) "The Administrative Challenge of the Iran Hostage Crisis," Paper presented at a Workshop on Crisis Decisionmaking, International Institute of Administrative Sciences, Brussels, Belgium, December 11-14.

William L. Waugh, Jr. (1989a) "Informing Policy and Administration: A Comparative Perspective on Terrorism," *International Journal of Public Administration* 12 (January).

William L. Waugh, Jr. (1989b) "Controlling Terrorism in the U.S.," Paper delivered to the Annual Meeting of the International Studies Association/British International Studies Association, University of London, London, England, March 27-April 2.

William L. Waugh, Jr. (1989c) "Emergency Management and State and Local Government Capacities," in *Cities and Disaster: North American Studies in Emergency Management*, edited by Richard T. Sylves and William L. Waugh, Jr. (Springfield, Ill.: Charles C. Thomas Publishers).

William H. Webster (1986) "Fighting Terrorism in the United States," in *Terrorism: How the West Can Win*, edited by Benjamin Netanyahu (New York: Farrar-Straus-Giroux).

Paul Wilkinson (1977) *Terrorism and the Liberal State* (New York: John Wiley and Sons).

Eric Willenz (1987) "U.S. Policy on Terrorism: In Search of an Answer," *Terrorism* 9: 225-240.

James E. Winkates (1989) "Toward a Western Counterterrorist Policy," Paper delivered at the Annual Meeting of the International Studies Association/British International Studies Association, University of London, London, England, March 29-April 1.

Chapter 6

MANAGING TERRORISM: SOME CONCLUSIONS AND RECOMMENDATIONS

The thesis of this analysis has been that an emergency management approach to the problem of terrorism may provide a framework for a more comprehensive and effective policy. It has been further suggested that problem definition and the organization of programs to address the problem of terrorism will have significant impacts on the effectiveness of the policies. Certainly, framing the problem of terrorism in terms of its broader impact, rather than simply in terms of resolving separate acts or campaigns of violence, does suggest that the design of policy and the structures of response should be significantly different than those common in most nations today.

One of the limiting factors in designing and gaining support for emergency management programs has been that policymakers and the public at-large tend to think of emergency or crisis management solely in terms of the direct response mechanisms. There is also some vague understanding that disaster planning is necessary, but the extent of preparation for potential disasters, the need to mitigate the effects of such catastrophes, and the real problems of recovery are seldom considered. The strongly negative public response to civil defense planning may be a product of that limited view of emergency management. Also, to develop such devastating scenarios as those of nuclear holocaust and to address the policy questions that they raise gives the scenarios some reality. In much the same way, the tendency is to view antiterrorism policies solely in terms of the military and law enforcement activities designed to resolve the incidents, rather than in terms of their broader implications and impacts. That predisposition to define the problem in limited terms suggests that simple, limited responses may be adequate. Conflicts arise when perceptions or values differ. Such was the case in the mid-1980s when television cameras focused on army tanks at Heathrow Airport in London and questions were raised concerning the possible loss of millions of dollars in tourism (Richter and Waugh, 1986).

Underlying the analysis has also been the idea that the organizational context of a nation's or community's antiterrorism responses inhibits flexibility and tends to define the problem in certain ways. In short, in structuring our antiterrorism (and counterterrorism) policies and programs as we have, we may have institutionalized a set of solutions that are both ineffective and inappropriate given the objectives of political leaders (see, Dery, 1984: 94-95; Katz and Kahn, 1966; Waugh, 1987 and 1989a) and the level of threat posed by the violence.

The emergency management framework is being proposed as a vehicle for redefining the policy problem raised by terrorist violence and broadening the focus of policies and programs intended to address it. "Terrorism" as it has been defined in Chapter 3 is in fact many kinds of violence. All the forms of terrorist violence outlined are characterized by common elements: the use or threat of extraordinary violence, the existence of political purposes or goals underlying the acts, the intent to have a psychological impact beyond the immediate victims, and the choice of victims for their symbolic (rather than instrumental) value (see: Waugh, 1982: 27). Notwithstanding those similarities, each form of terrorism manifests important characteristics that should affect how it is addressed. The policies and actions designed to resolve specific terrorist crises, such as barricade and hostage incidences or threatened bombings, can be fit into the broader policy framework. In short, officials should recognize and respond to the unique aspects of the violent events, but they should be aware of how those actions fit into the larger antiterrorism program.

The focus here has been on the potential for terrorists to cause catastrophic damage to life and property. If catastrophic, mass casualty and/or mass destruction, terrorism presents essentially the same kinds of challenges to responding agencies as other types of disasters and hazards, the same kinds of disaster programs may be appropriate. To the extent that there is a real potential for terrorist violence to become catastrophic in its effects, given the destructive capacities of modern weapons, the nihilistic motivations of some terrorist groups, and/or the fragility of modern society, policymakers should be preparing for that eventuality.

In terms of the emergency management framework, what has been suggested is that antiterrorism programs should be reasonably comprehensive and include programs to prepare for, mitigate the effects of, and recover from the destruction that might occur, as well as respond directly to the more immediate crises caused by the violence. Certainly, terrorism may take the form of a biological threat or nuclear accident or major structural failure. In that regard, the management of terrorism should be very similar to the management of those other events.

There are also similarities between the conflicts over interpretations of terrorism and appropriate responses and the scientific and political conflicts over the definition of other kinds of hazards. The assessments of hazards of all types are subject to disagreement, particularly as regards the extent of the risk that they pose (Waugh, 1988). The debate over the threat of terrorism is more and more frequently preceeded by the observation that it is not a serious problem when compared with other threats, except in terms of the potential for large scale violence, e.g., biological or nuclear terrorism. It is true for Americans that one is more likely to be killed in an automobile on the way to the

airport than killed by a terrorist during one's flight. It is also true
that ordinary Americans are more likely to die from lightning
strikes, shark attacks, and bathtub accidents. It is for that reason
that an emergency management perspective may be more appropriate than a more limited view and response. To the extent that
such violence may continue and become even more commonplace
than it is now, the emergency management perspective may help
institutionalize a set of responses to address the problem in its
numerous forms.

TERRORISM AND THE EMERGENCY MANAGEMENT PERSPECTIVE

The emergency management perspective is valuable for several
reasons. First, it assumes the threat to be somewhat unpredictable,
with tremendous variability in possible intensity - not unlike our
experience with terrorism. While scientists are developing the
requisite knowledge to anticipate the occurrence and intensity of
some catastrophic natural disasters, such as volcanic eruptions
and earthquakes, prediction is still not a reliable skill. As a
consequence of that unpredictability, the level of preparation for
such events needs to be adequate to respond to the worst case, or
nearly so. In reality, the preparation is only as adequate as public
support permits, unless preparation for more salient disaster-
types has utility for terrorism-related disasters.

Second, the perspective suggests that policies and programs
designed to address the threat of terrorism should be comprehensive. That is, they should be focused on the broad range of
activities that may be required to mitigate, prepare for, respond
to, and recover from the effects of a catastrophic terrorist incident,
rather than be simply focused on the response phase. The
development of the Integrated Emergency Management System
(IEMS) takes the preparation a step further as it is predicated on
the development and maintenance of a comprehensive set of
programs.

Third, to the extent that terrorism is a commonplace phenomenon, the routinization of antiterrorism programs would resolve some of the problems of legal jurisdiction and facilitate inter-agency and intergovernmental coordination in disaster responses. That is not to say, however, that emergency managers have solved the jurisdiction and coordination problems for other kinds of disaster programs. What it would mean is that the range of emergency management programs now in place could be brought to bear on terrorism-related hazards and disasters more easily. As in the cases of hurricanes, earthquakes, and other disasters, the agencies responsible for the responses to terrorist-sponsored catastrophes will also be concerned about the implications that a particular response will have for future mitigation, preparedness, and recovery activities. The broader perspective would have a significant impact on the way that terrorist threats are handled. For one thing immediate threats to life and property would likely take precedence over possible future threats, although the potential for future losses would not be ignored by decision-makers.

Fourth, the emergency management perspective may also suggest other fruitful areas of policymaking, other solutions to the problem of terrorism or at least new means to mitigate its effects. Indeed, analysts and scholars are suggesting that the nature of the terrorism problem is changing, with the violence becoming potentially more destructive and with terrorist organizations exhibiting less concern about public opinion and more willingness to sacrifice lives for political ends. At minimum, emergency managers may provide a last line of defense. The broader perspective, too, may facilitate the development of mitigation programs, such as encouraging security-sensitive construction and less vulnerable public facilities like mass transit networks.

Fifth, adoption of the perspective may well provide a clearer set of policy objectives. Typically, emergency managers are principally concerned with minimizing threats to and loss of life and property. While there may be political objectives as well, emergency management tends to focus on the routinization of reasonable precautions and preparations. That may not address the political problem of regimes needing to demonstrate the capacity and legitimacy of their institutions, but that imperative is an uncommon one among developed and developing nations.

Sixth, an emergency management perspective may increase the salience of the antiterrorism issue. In that salience is related to the frequency of occurrance, having a broadly focused emergency management effort means that support does not hinge on the importance that the public and public officials place on one kind of disaster. All-hazard programs benefit to some extent from any disaster occurrence.

It has also been suggested that the domination of the terrorism-related emergency management programs by military and law enforcement authorities may be problemmatic. The objectives of military and law enforcement decisionmakers may not be appropriate, in other words. While the adoption of law enforcement methods by Western European and U.S. governments in responding to international terrorist violence does appear to offer some promise, new organizational arrangements may suggest new solutions. A recent study of professional emergency managers in the U.S., for example, associated success in managing disasters with relevant professional expertise, ability to coordinate emergency management activities among a diverse set of agencies without attempting to dictate policy, and communication skills, among other qualities (Drabek, 1987). The successful emergency manager was described as a diplomat or mediator, rather than an authoritarian leader, because of the need to integrate the efforts of many agencies (each having its own jurisdiction and responsibilities) and reconcile the interests of many officials within and outside of the government.

THE MODELS OF TERRORISM AND POLICYMAKING

It has further been suggested that the perspective taken on terrorist violence is rooted in a set of fundamental assumptions about the nature and course of the violence. Those assumptions may be well-founded, but they also may not be. The threat that terrorism poses to the U.S. is similar to the threat posed to Israel only in terms of the violent nature of the phenomenon. Regardless of the nature of the terrorist organizations perpetrating the violence, both nations are not equally threatened. The U.S. is simply not as vulnerable to internal disruption and external coercion as Israel is. Nonetheless, American and Israeli antiterrorism policies have been essentially the same.

The distinction between revolutionary terrorism and other forms is primarily significant when the potential for revolution exists and the responding authorities need to identify possible terrorist targets. Without the potential for revolution, violence is violence and it may or may not be a significant military threat. Unless terrorists pose a credible threat to regime or societal stability, it will be counterproductive to respond to their activities as if they did pose such a threat. To overreact is to give them greater status than they merit.

Similarly, policies designed to address the kinds of threats posed by revolutionary terrorists may be counterproductive when applied to threats posed by vigilante terrorists. The models of terrorism described in Chapter 3 are predicated on the assumption that the political objectives of terrorist organizations, as well as governments, may differ and those differences should affect the choice of antiterrorism policies. The extent to which outside or foreign interests may be involved directly or indirectly in terrorist violence and increase its potency should affect government responses. The nature of the terrorist organization is also important, i.e., policymakers should determine whether the terrorists are representing (officially or not) incumbent elites and whether they are related to other political interests (including legitimate political parties, interest groups, ethnic groups, etc.). Terrorist objectives, however, are only as important as they are realistic, have potential for attracting domestic and/or international support, and facilitate the identification of potential targets of violence. The resilience of the target society, i.e., whether it can continue functioning and repair itself despite the violence, is also a major factor to consider in developing an appropriate response.

Clearly, the success of Western European governments with

their routinization of antiterrorism responses, particularly using police rather than military forces, supports the idea that the model of terrorism on which policy is based can determine the effectiveness of that policy. It is not presumed that the models in Chapter 3 represent all perspectives. However, the models are intended to make important points:

1. There are many forms of terrorism,
2. Several major interpretations of terrorist violence have tended to dominate policymaking, and
3. There is a compelling need to find an appropriate fit between the nature of the hazard that the violence presents and the policy options chosen.

In that regard, the assignment of agency responsibilities for U.S. national security preparedness policy, provided in Presidential Executive Order 12656 (see the Appendix), would seemingly be appropriate only for those acts of violence that have such catastrophic effects that the stability and function of the American government would be affected, such as a nuclear war. The concern with "continuity of government" reflects the seriousness of the disasters that the policy is designed to address. Little short of a nuclear attack on one or several American cities or a major biological attack that affects food supplies and/or heavily populated areas would be sufficient to put the machinery described into motion.

AN EMERGENCY MANAGEMENT FRAMEWORK FOR ANTITERRORISM PROGRAMS

An initial conclusion is that antiterrorism policies should give adequate consideration to the need for disaster preparedness, hazard or risk mitigation, and disaster recovery, as well as emergency response. The four-stage emergency management model offers that much framework. Similarly, the Integrated Emergency Management System (IEMS) model focuses on the need to conduct hazard analyses, capability assessments, and emergency planning as preparation for emergency responses and in anticipation of recovery efforts. The IEMS model also underscores the need to maintain response capabilities. Emergency preparedness and mitigation are ongoing activities, rather than simply discrete actions requiring only periodic review and update. The framework calls for more than bound and shelved emergency plans. The IEMS model outlined functions designed to assess, maintain, and upgrade emergency management capabilities so that nations or communities are as adequately prepared as possible.

The major problem identified in that discussion is that of limited regional (e.g., state, province, or district) and local government capacities to develop and maintain effective emergency management programs (Waugh, 1989b). Despite efforts to provide antiterrorism or counterterrorism training, intelligence, and some financial support, it is uncertain that local officials will have the wherewithal to respond effectively to large-scale terrorist incidents, even if only for the period of time prior to the arrival of federal or state antiterrorism forces. Additional obstacles to effective action, limiting capacities to respond to terrorism and other hazards, are posed by the vertical fragmentation of responsibilities under federal and even unitary systems of government, horizontal fragmentation of responsibilities typical of local governments and even agency jurisdictions within the same governments, and limited technical expertise and fiscal resources at all levels of government. The biggest question, however, may be whether state and local authorities have the political wherewithal to address the hazards posed by terrorism. The record has been mixed in regard to local government willingness and ability to regulate land use and construction to mitigate the effects of potential natural disasters (see, e.g., Baker and McPhie, 1975; Baram, 1981; Rossi, Wright, and Weber-Burdin, 1982; Drabek, Mushkatel, and Kilijanik, 1983; Feigenbaum and Ford, 1984; Godschalk and Brower, 1985; Clary, 1985; May and Williams, 1986) even when catastrophe has been imminent, plan effectively for long-term programs (see, e.g., Healy, 1969; Council of State

Governments, 1976; Foster, 1980; Waugh, 1988), and provide
financial support for even a minimal level of preparation for
potential disasters is more often lacking than not (see, e.g.,
Kunreuther, 1973; Dacy and Kunreuther, 1979; Waugh, 1989b). To
implement an effective emergency management system for
possible terrorist (as well as other) catastrophes, it will be
necessary to overcome the obstacles common to emergency
management in general and to terrorism in particular.

DESIGNING AN EFFECTIVE EMERGENCY MANAGEMENT
MECHANISM

Overcoming the obstacles to effective action will not be easy.
While terrorism has had considerable salience as an issue over the
past three decades, that public interest has tended to wane during
periods of relative inactivity. The public has apparently adjusted
to the security programs at airports and in public buildings, albeit
with only occasional exhibits of frustration. That familiarity,
however, breeds complacency and educational campaigns are
necessary to renew understanding of the danger and of the nature
of the antiterrorism technologies. The level of public interest in
antiterrorism programs, too, may wane as the salience of national
security issues wane. Recent changes in the relations between East
and West are leading to debates in Western European and the
U.S., as well as elsewhere, concerning levels of defense spending.
Tying antiterrorism programs to broader emergency management
programs may well increase the salience of all the programs.
    The current weakness of political and administrative con-
stituencies for antiterrorism programs can be alleviated somewhat by the broadening of the policy framework. If terrorism is
viewed as a common problem involving political leaders and
professional emergency managers at all levels of government,
rather than an issue largely within the purview of the central
government's law enforcement and national security apparatus,
the antiterrorism effort will enjoy greater political and administrative support. To some extent that is being done in the U.S.

through the education and training programs of the Federal Bureau of Investigation, but there is clear federal domination of the intergovernmental relationships so developed.

The development of broad political and administrative constituencies will also reduce friction caused by fragmented governmental structures and increase regional, state, and local capacities to respond to the potential of terrorism. Technical assistance, training, and fiscal transfers can increase the administrative, fiscal, and political capacities of those authorities to act effectively. Capacity to respond seldom increases when a higher authority assumes responsibility for responding to disasters (e.g., see Stallings and Schepart, 1989).

Little can be done to change the fiscal climate and emergency management programs of all kinds do not fare well in the budgetary process when monies are scarce. Nevertheless, the capacities of local agencies to respond effectively can generally be enhanced considerably with minimal infusions of money. That has been the experience with other disaster preparedness programs in the U.S.

Having offered some recommendations based on the experience with natural and other man-made disasters, it must be noted that terrorism poses several other problems. Some are unique to antiterrorism policymaking and programs and others are common to many disaster-types. Unlike most of the disaster-types with which emergency managers deal, terrorism involves events precipitated by man against man. That being the case, part of the dilemma in responding to terrorism is anticipating the actions of other men and dissuading them from their violence. Negotiation and intimidation are not common to other kinds of disaster responses. Notwithstanding that difference, the emergency management framework can accommodate the unique nature of antiterrorism responses.

The political nature of terrorism (in the forms addressed here) is not necessarily unique, except to the extent that it does represent the rational action of men. As in responding to terrorism, natural and man-made disasters do attract political figures seeking to enhance their images as decisive, effective, and even brave leaders. Emergency managers have learned to remove operational decisionmaking to a central but isolated location, away from the demands of "uninvolved" political leaders and the media, and to structure the release of information to the public to minimize fear and maximize credibility. Political executives are called upon to reassure the public and to communicate essential information for the emergency management effort, at least in theory. By contrast, terrorist events are frequently characterized by the impassioned rhetoric of political leaders that increases the emotional content of the events and reduces the range of options available to those responding to the crisis. That involvement of high level political leaders has a profound impact on the resolution of the crisis at-hand. As a result, it has been suggested that presidents and prime ministers not be involved directly in the resolution of terrorist incidents and particularly not be quick to magnify the impact of the events through media exposure. To command the attention of the nation's head of state or government is frequently a terrorist objective.

Having said that, it is clear that there is a political imperative for political leaders to appear strong and effective. That imperative may be more compelling in some nations than in others, just as risk is viewed differently (Jasanoff, 1986). It is uncertain that the public will be willing to be confined to press releases and news conferences by bureaucrats in the lead emergency management agency, at least initially. While there has been some public demand for demonstrations of political leadership during natural and technological disasters, there does seem to be more willingness to accept the judgment and actions of professional emergency managers.

What is being recommended is that antiterrorism policies be built around the emergency management framework with the law enforcement and national security authorities responsible for resolving immediate crises and developing response plans as only one component in that larger organization. Using an institution like the Federal Emergency Management Agency (FEMA) as the focal point or even lead agency in designing, implementing, and maintaining the set of antiterrorism policies and program would seen logical and, in some measure, is what is being done in the U.S. That agency does present some political problems, however, in terms of its association with the Department of Defense, its unfortunate administrative history, and the heavy-handedness which has characterized many of its operations. A similar agency, less oriented toward civil defense and more oriented toward natural and man-made disasters, would provide better balance for policymaking. To the extent that we are dealing with catastrophic disasters here, there will certainly be national security implications. But the need is to balance them out with other national interests.

As in the discussion of effective professional emergency managers, the principal task may be in designing a system that clearly delineates agency responsibilities with one lead agency responsible for coordinating, but not necessarily controlling, the antiterrorism program. The emphasis should be on concensus building rather than on hierarchical control. Decentralized decisionmaking is to be expected and agreement on goals and objectives will assure greater consistency in the decisions made.

Moreover, it is unlikely (even inconceivable) that one level of government or one agency will have clear jurisdiction over a major terrorist-spawned disaster. Indeed, it is unlikely given the fragmented nature of government in most large developed nations that one agency could adequately design, implement, operate and maintain programs to prepare for, mitigate the effects of, respond to, and recover from disasters without involving other agencies. Coordination of efforts, therefore, is a fundamental concern and professional networks are essential.

Terrorism is expected to remain with us for the foreseeable future. While experts are divided on the issue of whether we can expect catastrophic acts of terrorism, few argue that terrorist groups lack the capacity to carry out such acts. Terrorism does pose a hazard, then. One course of action is to develop a narrowly focused set of antiterrorism and counterterrorism programs as many nations are already doing. A second course is to make best use of current emergency management resources to develop a broader focused network of policies and programs that will address the range of problems that terrorist violence might engender. The emergency management framework provides just such a focus.

REFERENCES

Earl T. Baker and Tae Gordon McPhie (1975) *Land Use Management and Regulation in Hazardous Areas*(Boulder, Colo.: University of Colorado, Institute of Behavioral Science, Monograph No. 6).

Michael Baram (1981) *Alternatives to Regulation: Managing Risks to Health, Safety and the Environment* (Lexington, Mass.: Lexington Books).

Bruce B. Clary (1985) "The Evolution and Structure of Natural Hazards Policies," *Pubic Administration Review* (Special Issue, 1985): 20-28.

Douglas Dacy and Howard Kunreuther (1979) *Economics of Disasters: Implications for Federal Policy* (New York: Free Press).

David Dery (1984) *Problem Definition in Policy Analysis*, with an Introduction by Aaron Wildavsky (Lawrence, Kansas: University of Kansas Press).

Thomas M. Dietz and Robert W. Rycroft (1987) *The Risk Professionals* (New York: Russell Sage Foundation).

Thomas E. Drabek (1987) *The Professional Emergency Manager: Structures and Strategies for Success* (Boulder, Colo.: University of Colorado, Institute of Behavioral Science, Program on Environment and Behavior Monograph No. 44).

Thomas E. Drabek (1983) *Earthquake Mitigation Policy: The Experience of Two States* (Boulder, Colo.: University of Colorado, Institute of Behavioral Science Publication No. 37).

Thomas E. Drabek, Harrett Tansminga, Thomas Kilijanik, and Christopher Adams (1981) *Managing Multiorganizational Emergency Responses* (Boulder, Colo.: University of Colorado, Institute of Behavioral Science Publication No. 6).

Edward D. Feigenbaum and Mark L. Ford (1984) *Emergency Management in the States* (Lexington, Ky.: Council of State Governments).

Harold D. Foster (1980) *Disaster Planning: Preservation of Life and Property* (New York: Springer-Verlag).

David R. Godschalk and David J. Brower (1985) "Mitigation Strategies and Integrated Emergency Management," *Public Administration Review* (Special Issue, 1985): 64-71.

Sheila Jasanoff (1986) *Risk Management and Political Culture* (New York: Russell Sage Foundation).

Daniel Katz and Robert L. Kahn (1966) *The Social Psychology of Organizations* (New York: Wiley and Sons).

Howard Kunreuther (1973) *Recovery from Natural Disasters: Insurance or Federal Aid?* (Washington, DC: American Enterprise Institute, Evaluation Studies #12).

Ralph G. Lewis (1988) "Management Issues in Emergency Response," pp. 163-179 in *Managing Disaster: Strategies and Policy Perspectives*, edited by Louise K. Comfort (Durham, NC: Duke University Press).

Peter J. May and Walter Williams (1986) *Disaster Policy Implementation: Managing Programs Under Shared Governance* (New York: Plenum Press).

William J. Petak and Arthur A. Atkisson (1982) *Natural Hazard Risk Assessment and Public Policy: Anticipating the Unexpected*(New York: Springer-Verlag).

Peter Rossi, James D. Wright, and Eleanor Weber-Burdin (1982) *Natural Hazards and Public Choice: The State and Local Politics of Hazard Mitigation* (New York: Academic Press).

Robert A. Stallings and Charles B. Schepart (1989) "Contrasting Local Government Responses to a Tornado Disaster in Two Communities," in *Cities and Disaster: North American Studies in Emergency Management*, edited by Richard T. Sylves and William L. Waugh, Jr. (Springfield, Ill.: Charles C. Thomas Publishers).

William L. Waugh, Jr. (1987) "The Administrative Challenge of the Iranian Hostage Crisis," Paper presented at the Workshop on "Crisis Decision Making: An International Perspective," International Institute of Administrative Sciences, Brussels, Belgium, December.

William L. Waugh, Jr. (1988) "Current Policy and Implementation Issues in Disaster Preparedness," pp. 111-125 in *Managing Disaster: Strategies and Policy Perspectives*, edited by Louise K. Comfort (Durham, NC: Duke University Press).

William L. Waugh, Jr. (1989a) "The Structure of Decisionmaking in the Iran Hostage Rescue Attempt," Paper presented at the Biannual Meeting of the International Association for Conflict Management, Athens, Georgia, June 12-14.

William L. Waugh, Jr. (1989b) "Emergency Management and the Capacities of State and Local Governments," in *Cities and Disaster: North American Studies in Emergency Management*, edited by Richard

T. Sylves and William L. Waugh, Jr. (Springfield, Ill.: Charles C. Thomas Publishers).

William L. Waugh, Jr. (1990) "Volcanic Hazards," in *Emergency Management Handbook*, edited by William L. Waugh, Jr., and Ronald John Hy (Westport, Conn: Greenwood Press).

Appendix

EXECUTIVE ORDER 12656, ASSIGNMENT OF EMERGENCY PREPAREDNESS RESPONSIBILITIES, NOVEMBER 18, 1988

Whereas our national security is dependent upon our ability to assure continuity of government, at every level, in any national security emergency situation that might confront the Nation; and

Whereas effective national preparedness planning to meet such an emergency, including a massive nuclear attack, is essential to our national survival; and

Whereas effective national preparedness planning requires the identification of functions that would have to be performed during such an emergency, the assignment of responsibility for developing plans for performing these functions, and the assignment of responsibility for developing the capability to implement these plans; and

Whereas the Congress has directed the development of such national security emergency preparedness plans and has provided funds for the accomplishment thereof:

Now, Therefore, by virtue of the authority vested in me as President by the Constitution and laws of the United States of America, and pursuant to Reorganization Plan No. 1 of 1958 (72 Stat. 1799), the National Security Act of 1947, as amended, the Defense Production Act of 1950, as amended, and the Federal Civil Defense Act, as amended, it is hereby ordered that the responsibilities of the Federal departments and agencies in national security emergencies shall be as follows:

PART 1 – PREAMBLE

Section 101. National Security Emergency Preparedness Policy.
(a) The policy of the United States is to have sufficient capabilities at all levels of government to meet essential defense and civilian needs during any national security emergency. A national security emergency is any occurrence, including natural disaster, military attack, technological emergency, or other emergency, that seriously degrades or seriously threatens the national security of the United States. Policy for national security emergency preparedness shall be established by the President. Pursuant to the President's direction, the National Security Council shall be responsible for developing and administering such policy. All national security emergency preparedness activities shall be consistent with the Constitution and laws of the United States and with preservation of the constitutional government of the United States.

(b) Effective national security emergency preparedness planning requires: identification of functions that would have to be performed during such an emergency; development of plans for performing these functions; and development of the capability to execute those plans.

Section 102. Purpose. (a) The purpose of this Order is to assign national security emergency preparedness responsibilities to Federal Departments and agencies. These assignments are based, whenever possible, on extensions of the regular missions of the departments and agencies.

(b) This Order does not constitute authority to implement the plans prepared pursuant to this Order. Plans so developed may be executed only in the event that authority for such extension is authorized by law.

Section 103. Scope.   (a) This Order addresses national security emergency preparedness functions and activities. As used in this Order, preparedness functions and activities include, as appropriate, policies, plans, procedures, and readiness measures that enhance the ability of the United States Government to mobilize for, respond to, and recover from a national security emergency.

(b) This Order does not apply to those natural disasters, technological emergencies, or other emergencies, the alleviation of which is normally the responsibility of individuals, the private sector, volunteer organizations, State and local governments, and Federal departments and agencies unless such situations also constitute a national security emergency.

(c) This Order does not require the provision of information concerning, or evaluation of, military policies, plans, programs, or states of military readiness.

(d) This Order does not apply to national security emergency preparedness telecommunications functions and responsibilities that are otherwise assigned by Executive Order 12472.

Section 104. Management of National Security Emergency Preparedness.   (a) The National Security Council is the principal forum for consideration of national security emergency preparedness policy.

(b) The National Security Council shall arrange for Executive branch liaison with, and assistance to, the Congress and the Federal judiciary on national security emergency preparedness matters.

(c) The Director of the Federal Emergency Management Agency shall serve as an advisor to the National Security Council on issues of national security emergency preparedness, including mobilization preparedness, civil defense, continuity of government, technological disasters, and other issues, as appropriate. Pursuant to such procedures for the organization and management of the National Security Council process as the President may establish, the Director of the Federal Emergency Management Agency also shall assist in the implementation of and management of the National Security Council process as the President may establish, the Director of the Federal Emergency Management Agency also shall assist in the implementation of national security emergency preparedness policy by coordinating with the other Federal departments and agencies and with State and local governments, and by providing periodic reports to the National Security Council on implementation of national security emergency preparedness policy.

(d) National security emergency preparedness functions that are shared by more than one agency shall be coordinated by the head of the Federal department or agency having primary responsibility and shall be supported by the heads of other departments and agencies having related responsibilities.

(e) There shall be a national security emergency exercise program that shall be supported by the heads of all appropriate Federal departments and agencies.

(f) Plans and procedures will be designed and developed to provide maximum flexibility to the President for his implementation of emergency actions.

Section 105. Interagency Coordination. (a) All appropriate Cabinet members and agency heads shall be consulted regarding national security emergency preparedness programs and policy issues. Each department and agency shall support interagency coordination to improve preparedness and response to a national security emergency and shall develop and maintain decentralized capabilities wherever feasible and appropriate.

(b) Each Federal department and agency shall work within the framework established by, and cooperate with those organizations assigned responsibility in, Executive Order 12472, to ensure adequate national security emergency preparedness telecommunications in support of the functions and activities addressed by this Order.

PART 2 – GENERAL PROVISIONS

Section 201. General. The head of each Federal department and agency, as appropriate, shall:

(1) Be prepared to respond adequately to all national security emergencies, including those that are international in scope, and those that may occur within any region of the Nation;

(2) Consider national security emergency preparedness factors in the conduct of his or her regular functions, particularly those functions essential in time of emergency. Emergency plans and programs, and an appropriate state of readiness, including organizational infrastructure, shall be developed as an integral part of the continuing activities of each Federal department and agency.

(3) Appoint a senior policy official as Emergency Coordinator, responsible for developing and maintaining a multi-year, national security emergency preparedness plan for the department or agency to include objectives, programs, and budgetary requirements.

(4) Design preparedness measures to permit a rapid and effective transition from routine to emergency operations, and to make effective use of the period following initial indication of a probable national security emergency. This will include:

(a) Development of a system of emergency actions that defines alternatives, processes, and issues to be considered during various states of national security emergencies;

(b) Identification of actions that could be taken in the early stages of a national security emergency or pending national security emergency to mitigate the impact of or reduce significantly the lead times associated with full emergency action implementation;

(5) Base national security emergency preparedness measures on the use of existing authorities, organizations, resources, and systems to the maximum extent practicable;

(6)   Identify areas where additional legal authorities may be needed to assist management and, consistent with applicable Executive orders, take appropriate measures toward acquiring those authorities.

(7)   Make policy recommendations to the National Security Council regarding national security emergency preparedness activities and functions of the Federal government;

(8)   Coordinate with State and local government agencies and other organizations, including private sector organizations, when appropriate. Federal plans should include appropriate involvement of and reliance upon private sector organizations in the response to national security emergencies;

(9)   Assist State, local, and private sector entities in developing plans for mitigating the effects of national security emergencies and for providing services that are essential to a national response;

(10)   Cooperate, to the extent appropriate, in compiling, evaluating, and exchanging relevant data related to all aspects of national security emergency preparedness;

(11)   Develop programs regarding congressional relations and public information that could be used during national security emergencies;

(12)   Ensure a capability to provide, during a national security emergency, information concerning Acts of Congress, presidential proclamations, Executive orders, regulations, and notices of other actions to the Archivist of the United States, for publication in the *Federal Register*, or to each agency designated to maintain the *Federal Register* in an emergency;

(13)   Develop and conduct training and education programs that incorporate emergency preparedness and civil defense information necessary to ensure an effective national response;

(14)   Ensure that plans consider the consequences for essential services provided by State and local governments, and by the private sector, if the flow of Federal funds is disrupted;

(15)   Consult and coordinate with the Director of the Federal Emergency Management Agency to ensure that those activities

and plans are consistent with current National Security Council guidelines and policies.

Section 202. Continuity of Government. The head of each Federal department and agency shall ensure the continuity of essential functions in any national security emergency by providing for: succession to office and emergency delegation of authority in accordance with applicable law; safekeeping of essential resources, facilities, and records; and establishment of emergency operating capabilities.

Section 203. Resource Management. The head of each Federal department and agency, as appropriate within assigned areas of responsibility, shall:

(1) Develop plans and programs to mobilize personnel (including reservist programs), equipment, facilities, and other resources;

(2) Assess essential emergency requirements and plan for the possible use of alternative resources to meet essential demands during and following national security emergencies;

(3) Prepare plans and procedures to share between and among the responsible agencies resources such as energy, equipment, food, land, materials, minerals, services, supplies, transportation, water, and workforce needed to carry out assigned responsibilities and other essential functions, and cooperate with other agencies in developing programs to ensure availability of such resources in a national security emergency;

(4) Develop plans to set priorities and allocate resources among civilian and military claimants;

(5) Identify occupations and skills for which there may be a critical need in the event of a national security emergency.

Section 204. Protection of Essential Resources and Facilities. The head of each Federal Department and agency, within assigned areas of responsibility, shall:

(1) Identify facilities and resources, both government and private, essential to the national defense and national welfare, and assess their vulnerabilities and develop strategies, plans, and

programs to provide for the security of such facilities and resources, and to avoid or minimize disruptions of essential services during any national security emergency;

(2) Participate in interagency activities to assess the relative importance of various facilities and resources to essential military and civilian needs and to integrate preparedness and response strategies and procedures;

(3) Maintain a capability to assess promptly the effect of attack and other disruptions during national security emergencies.

Section 205. Federal Benefit, Insurance, and Loan Programs. The head of each Federal department and agency that administers a loan, insurance, or benefit program that relies upon the Federal government payment system shall coordinate with the Secretary of the Treasury in developing plans for the continuation or restoration, to the extent feasible, of such programs in national security emergencies.

Section 206. Research. The Director of the Office of Science and Technology Policy and the heads of Federal departments and agencies having significant research and development programs shall advise the National Security Council of scientific and technological developments that should be considered in national security emergency preparedness planning.

Section 207. Redelegation. The head of each Federal department and agency is hereby authorized, to the extent otherwise permitted by law, to redelegate the functions assigned by this Order, and to authorize successive redelegations to organizations, officers, or employees within that department or agency.

Section 208. Transfer of Functions. Recommendations for interagency transfer of any emergency preparedness function assigned under this Order or for assignment of any new emergency preparedness function shall be coordinated with all affected Federal departments and agencies before submission to the National Security Council.

Section 209. Retention of Existing Authority. Nothing in this Order shall be deemed to derogate from assignments of functions to any Federal department or agency or officer thereof made by law.

PART 3 – DEPARTMENT OF AGRICULTURE

Section 301. Lead Responsibilities. In addition to the applicable responsibilities covered in Parts 1 and 2, the Secretary of Agriculture shall:

(1) Develop plans to provide for the continuation of agricultural production, food processing, storage, and distribution through the wholesale level in national security emergencies, and to provide for the domestic distribution of seed, feed, fertilizer, and farm equipment to agricultural producers;

(2) Develop plans to provide food and agricultural products to meet international responsibilities in national security emergencies;

(3) Develop plans and procedures for administration and use of Commodity Credit Corporation inventories of food and fiber resources in national security emergencies;

(4) Develop plans for the use of resources under the jurisdiction of the Secretary of Agriculture and, in cooperation with the Secretaries of Commerce, Defense, and the Interior, the Board of Directors of the Tennessee Valley Authority, and the heads of other government entities, plan for the national security emergency management, production, and processing of forest products;

(5) Develop, in coordination with the Secretary of Defense, plans and programs for water to be used in agricultural production and food processing in national security emergencies;

(6) In cooperation with Federal, State, and local agencies, develop plans for a national program relating to the prevention and control of fires in rural areas of the United States caused by the effects of enemy attack or other national security emergencies;

(7) Develop plans to help provide the Nation's farmers with

production resources, including national security emergency financing capabilities;

(8) Develop plans, in consonance with those of the Department of Health and Human Services, the Department of the Interior, and the Environmental Protection Agency, for national security emergency agricultural health services and forestry, including:

(a) Diagnosis and control or eradication of diseases, pests, or hazardous agents (biological, chemical, or radiological) against animals, crops, timber, or products thereof;

(b) Protection, treatment, and handling of livestock and poultry, or products thereof, that have been exposed to or affected by hazardous agents;

(c) Use and handling of crops, agricultural commodities, timber, and agricultural lands that have been exposed to or affected by hazardous agents; and

(d) Assuring the safety and wholesomeness, and minimizing losses from hazards, of animals and animal products and agricultural commodities and products subject to continuous inspection by the Department of Agriculture or owned by the Commodity Credit Corporation or by the Department of Agriculture;

(9) In consultation with the Secretary of State and the Director of the Federal Emergency Management Agency, represent the United States in agriculture-related international civil emergency preparedness planning and related activities.

Section 302. Support Responsibility. The Secretary of Agriculture shall assist the Secretary of Defense in formulating and carrying out plans for stockpiling strategic and critical agricultural materials.

PART 4 – DEPARTMENT OF COMMERCE

Section 401. Lead Responsibilities. In addition to the applicable responsibilities covered in Parts 1 and 2, the Secretary of Commerce shall:

(1) Develop control systems for priorities, allocation, production, and distribution of materials and other resources that will be available to support both national defense and essential civilian programs in a national security emergency;

(2) In cooperation with the Secretary of Defense and other departments and agencies, identify those industrial products and facilities that are essential to mobilization readiness, national defense, or post-attack survival and recovery;

(3) In cooperation with the Secretary of Defense and other Federal departments and agencies, analyze potential effects of national security emergencies on actual production capability, taking into account the entire production complex, including shortages of resources, and develop preparedness measures to strengthen capabilities for production increases in national security emergencies;

(4) In cooperation with the Secretary of Defense, perform industry analyses to assess capabilities of the commercial industrial base to support the national defense, and develop policy alternatives to improve the international competitiveness of specific domestic industries and their abilities to meet defense program needs;

(5) In cooperation with the Secretary of the Treasury, develop plans for providing emergency assistance to the private sector through direct or participation loans for the financing of production facilities and equipment;

(6) In cooperation with the Secretaries of State, Defense, Transportation, and the Treasury, prepare plans to regulate and control exports and imports in national security emergencies;

(7) Provide for the collection and reporting of census information on human and economic resources, and maintain a capability to conduct emergency surveys to provide information on the status of these resources as required for national security purposes;

(8) Develop overall plans and programs to ensure that the fishing industry continues to produce and process essential protein in national security emergencies;

(9) Develop plans to provide meteorological, hydrologic,

marine weather, geodetic, hydrographic, climatic, seismic, and oceanographic data and services to Federal, State, and local agencies, as appropriate;

(10) In coordination with the Secretary of State and the Director of the Federal Emergency Management Agency, represent the United States in industry-related international (NATO and allied) civil emergency preparedness planning and related activities.

Section 402. Support Responsibilities.   The Secretary of Commerce shall:

(1) Assist the Secretary of Defense in formulating and carrying out plans for stockpiling strategic and critical materials;   (2) Support the Secretary of Agriculture in planning for the national security management, production, and processing of forest and fishery products;

(3) Assist, in consultation with the Secretaries of State and Defense, the Secretary of the Treasury in the formulation and execution of economic measures affecting other nations.

PART 5 – DEPARTMENT OF DEFENSE

Section 501. Lead Responsibilities.   In addition to the applicable responsibilities covered in Parts 1 and 2, the Secretary of Defense shall:

(1)   Ensure military preparedness and readiness to respond to national security emergencies;

(2)   In coordination with the Secretary of Commerce, develop, with industry, government, and the private sector, reliable capabilities for the rapid increase of defense production to include industrial resources required for that production;

(3)   Develop and maintain, in cooperation with the heads of other departments and agencies, national security emergency plans, programs, and mechanisms to ensure effective mutual support between and among the military, civil government, and the private sector;

(4)   Develop and maintain damage assessment capabilities

and assist the Director of the Federal Emergency Management Agency and the heads of other departments and agencies in developing and maintaining capabilities to assess attack damage and to estimate the effects of potential attack on the Nation;

(5)   Arrange, through agreements with the heads of other Federal departments and agencies, for the transfer of certain Federal resources to the jurisdiction and/or operational control of the Department of Defense in national security emergencies;

(6)   Acting through the Secretary of the Army, develop, with the concurrence of the heads of all affected departments and agencies, overall plans for the management, control, and allocation of of all usable waters from all sources within the jurisdiction of the United States. This includes:

(a)   Coordination of national security emergency water resource planning at the national, regional, State, and local levels;

(b)   Development of plans to assure emergency provision of water from public works projects under the jurisdiction of the Secretary of the Army to public water supply utilities and critical defense production facilities during national security emergencies;

(c)   Development of plans to assure emergency operation of waterways and harbors; and

(d)   Development of plans to assure the provision of potable water;

(7)   In consultation with the Secretaries of State and Energy, the Director of the Federal Emergency Management Agency, and others, as required, develop plans and capabilities for identifying, analyzing, mitigating, and responding to hazards related to nuclear weapons, materials, and devices; and maintain liaison, as appropriate, with the Secretary of Energy and the Members of the Nuclear Regulatory Commission to ensure the continuity of nuclear weapons production and the appropriate allocation of scarce resources, including the recapture of special nuclear materials from Nuclear Regulatory Commission licensees when appropriate;

(8) Coordinate with the Administrator of the National Aeronautics and Space Administration and the Secretary of Energy, as appropriate, to prepare for the use, maintenance, and development of technologically advanced aerospace and aeronautical-related systems, equipment, and methodologies applicable to national security emergencies;

(9) Develop, in coordination with the Secretary of Labor, the Directors of the Selective Service System, the Office of Personnel Management, and the Federal Emergency Management Agency, plans and systems to ensure that the Nation's human resources are available to meet essential military and civilian needs in national security emergencies;

(10) Develop national security emergency operational procedures, and coordinate with the Secretary of Housing and Urban Development with respect to residential property, for the control, acquisition, leasing, assignment and priority of occupancy of real property with the jurisdiction of the Department of Defense;

(11) Review the priorities and allocations systems developed by other departments and agencies to ensure that they meet Department of Defense needs in a national security emergency; and develop and maintain the Department of Defense programs necessary for effective utilization of all priorities and allocations systems;

(12) Develop, in coordination with the Attorney General of the United States, specific procedures by which military assistance to civilian law enforcement authorities may be requested, considered, and provided;

(13) In cooperation with the Secretary of Commerce and other departments and agencies, identify those industrial products and facilities that are essential to mobilization readiness, national defense, or post-attack survival and recovery;

(14) In cooperation with the Secretary of Commerce and other Federal departments and agencies, analyze potential effects of national security emergencies on actual production capability, taking into account the entire production complex, including shortages of resources, and develop preparedness measures to strengthen capabilities for production increases in national security emergencies;

(15) With the assistance of the heads of other Federal departments and agencies, provide management direction for the stockpiling of strategic and critical materials, conduct storage, maintenance, and quality assurance operations for the stockpile of strategic and critical materials, and reports relating to the stockpiling of strategic and critical materials.

Section 502. Support Responsibilities. The Secretary of Defense shall:

(1) Advise and assist the heads of other Federal departments and agencies in the development of plans and programs to support national mobilization. This includes providing, as appropriate:

(a) Military requirements, prioritized and time-phased to the extent possible, for selected end-items and supporting services, materials, and components;

(b) Recommendations for use of financial incentives and other methods to improve defense production as provided by law; and

(c) Recommendations for export and import policies;

(2) Advise and assist the Secretary of State and the heads of other Federal departments and agencies, as appropriate, in planning for the protection, evacuation, and repatriation of United States citizens in threatened areas overseas;

(3) Support the Secretary of Housing and Urban Development and the heads of other agencies, as appropriate, in the development of plans to restore community facilities;

(4) Support the Secretary of Energy in international liaison activities pertaining to nuclear materials facilities;

(5) In consultation with the Secretaries of State and Commerce, assist the Secretary of the Treasury in the formulation and execution of economic measures that affect other nations;

(6) Support the Secretary of State and the heads of other Federal departments and agencies as appropriate in the formulation and implementation of foreign policy, and the negotiation of

contingency and post-emergency plans, intergovernmental agreements, and arrangements with allies and friendly nations, which affect national security;

(7) Coordinate with the Director of the Federal Emergency Management Agency the development of plans for mutual civil-military support during national security emergencies;

(8) Develop plans to support the Secretary of Labor in providing education and training to overcome shortages of critical skills.

PART 6 – DEPARTMENT OF EDUCATION

Section 601. Lead Responsibilities.   In addition to the applicable responsibilities covered in Parts 1 and 2, the Secretary of Education shall:

(1) Assist school systems in developing their plans to provide for the earliest possible resumption of activities following national security emergencies;

(2) Develop plans to provide assistance, including efforts to meet shortages of critical educational personnel, to local educational agencies;

(3) Develop plans, in coordination with the Director of the Federal Emergency Management Agency, for dissemination of emergency preparedness instructional materials through educational institutions and the media during national security emergencies.

Section 602. Support Responsibilities.   The Secretary of Education shall:

(1) Develop plans to support the Secretary of Labor in providing education and training to overcome shortages of critical skills;

(2) Support the Secretary of Health and Human Services in the development of human services educational and training materials, including self-help program materials for use by human service organizations and professional schools.

PART 7 – DEPARTMENT OF ENERGY

Section 701. Lead Responsibilities. In addition to the applicable responsibilities covered in Parts 1 and 2, the Secretary of Energy shall:

(1)   Conduct national security emergency preparedness planning, including capabilities development, and administer operational programs for all energy resources, including:

    (a)   Providing information, in cooperation with Federal, State, and energy industry officials, on energy supply and demand conditions and on the requirements for and the availability of materials and services critical to energy supply systems;

    (b)   In coordination with appropriate departments and agencies and in consultation with the energy industry, develop implementation plans and operational systems for priorities and allocation of all energy resource requirements for national defense and essential civilian needs to assure national security emergency preparedness;

    (c)   Developing, in consultation with the Board of Directors of the Tennessee Valley Authority, plans necessary for the integration of its power system into the national supply system;

(2)   Identify energy facilities essential to the mobilization, deployment, and sustainment of resources to support the national security and national welfare, and develop energy supply and demand strategies to ensure continued provision of minimum essential services in national security emergencies;

(3) In coordination with the Secretary of Defense, ensure continuity of nuclear weapons production consistent with national security requirements;

(4)   Assure the security of nuclear materials, nuclear weapons, or devices in the custody of the Department of Energy, as well as the security of all other Department of Energy programs and facilities;

(5) In consultation with the Secretaries of State and Defense and the Director of the Federal Emergency Management Agency, conduct appropriate international liaison activities pertaining to matters within the jurisdiction of the Department of Energy;

(6) In consultation with the Secretaries of State and Defense, the Director of the Federal Emergency Management Agency, the Members of the Nuclear Regulatory Commission, and others, as required, develop plans and capabilities for identification, analysis, damage assessment, and mitigation of hazards from nuclear weapons, materials, and devices;

(7) Coordinate with the Secretary of Transportation in the planning and management of transportation resources involved in the bulk movement of energy;

(8) At the request of or with the concurrence of the Nuclear Regulatory Commission and in consultation with the Secretary of Defense, recapture special nuclear materials from Nuclear Regulatory Commission licensees where necessary to assure the use, preservation, or safeguarding of such material for the common defense and security;

(9) Develop national security emergency operational procedures for the control, utilization, acquisition, leasing, assignment, and priority of occupancy of real property within the jurisdiction of the Department of Energy;

(10) Manage all emergency planning and response activities pertaining to Department of Energy nuclear facilities.

Section 702. Support Responsibilities. The Secretary of Energy shall:

(1) Provide advice and assistance, in coordination with appropriate agencies, to Federal, State, and local officials and private sector organizations to assess the radiological impact associated with national security emergencies;

(2) Coordinate with the Secretaries of Defense and the Interior regarding the operation of hydroelectric projects to assure maximum energy output;

(3) Support the Secretary of Housing and Urban Development and the heads of other agencies, as appropriate, in the development of plans to restore community facilities;

(4) Coordinate with the Secretary of Agriculture regarding the emergency preparedness of the rural electric supply systems throughout the National and the assignment of emergency preparedness responsibilities to the Rural Electrification Administration.

PART 8 – DEPARTMENT OF HEALTH AND HUMAN SERVICES

Section 801. Lead Responsibilities. In addition to the applicable responsibilities covered in Parts 1 and 2, the Secretary of Health and Human Services shall:

(1) Develop national plans and programs to mobilize the health industry and health resources for the provision of health, mental health, and medical services in national security emergencies;

(2) Promote the development of State and local plans and programs for provision of health, mental health, and medical services in national security emergencies;

(3) Develop national plans to set priorities and allocate health, mental health, and medical services resources among civilian and military claimants;

(4) Develop health and medical survival information programs and a nationwide program to train health and mental health professionals and paraprofessionals in special knowledge and skills that would be useful in national security emergencies;

(5) Develop programs to reduce or eliminate adverse health and mental health effects produced by hazardous agents (biological, chemical, or radiological), and, in coordination with appropriate Federal agencies, develop programs to minimize property and environmental damage associated with national security emergencies;

(6) Develop guidelines that will assure reasonable and prudent standards of purity and/or safety in the manufacture and distribution of food, drugs, biological products, medical devices, food additives, and radiological products in national security emergencies;

(7) Develop national plans for assisting State and local governments in rehabilitation of persons injured or disabled during national security emergencies;

(8) Develop plans and procedures to assist State and local governments in the provision of emergency human services, including lodging, feeding, clothing, registration and inquiry, social services, family reunification and mortuary services and interment;

(9) Develop, in coordination with the Secretary of Education, human services educational and training materials for use by human service organizations and professional schools; and develop and distribute, in coordination with the Director of the Federal Emergency Management Agency, civil defense information relative to emergency human services;

(10) Develop plans and procedures, in coordination with the heads of Federal departments and agencies, for assistance to United States citizens or others evacuated from overseas areas.

Section 802. Support Responsibility. The Secretary of Health and Human Services shall support the Secretary of Agriculture in the development of plans related to national security emergency agricultural health services.

PART 9 – DEPARTMENT OF HOUSING AND URBAN DEVELOPMENT

Section 901. Lead Responsibilities. In addition to the applicable responsibilities covered in Parts 1 and 2, the Secretary of Housing and Urban Development shall:

(1) Develop plans for provision and management of housing in national security emergencies, including:

(a) Providing temporary housing using Federal financing and other arrangements;
(b) Providing for radiation protection by encouraging voluntary construction of shelters and voluntary use of

cost-efficient design and construction techniques to maximize population protection;

(2)   Develop plans, in cooperation with the heads of other Federal departments and agencies and State and local governments, to restore community facilities, including electrical power, potable water, and sewage disposal facilities, damaged in national security emergencies.

PART 10 – DEPARTMENT OF THE INTERIOR

Section 1001. Lead Responsibilities.   In addition to the applicable responsibilities covered in Parts 1 and 2, the Secretary of the Interior shall:

(1)   Develop programs and encourage the exploration, development, and mining of strategic and critical and other nonfuel minerals for national security emergency purposes;

(2)   Provide guidance to mining industries in the development of plans and programs to ensure continuity of production during national security emergencies;

(3)   Develop and implement plans for the management, control, allocation, and use of public land under the jurisdiction of the Department of the Interior in national security emergencies and coordinate land emergency planning at the Federal, State, and local levels.

Section 1002. Support Responsibilities.   The Secretary of the Interior shall:

(1)   Assist the Secretary of Defense in formulating and carrying out plans for stockpiling strategic and critical minerals;

(2)   Cooperate with the Secretary of Commerce in the identification and evaluation of facilities essential for national security emergencies;

(3)   Support the Secretary of Agriculture in planning for the national security management, production, and processing of forest products.

PART 11 – DEPARTMENT OF JUSTICE

Section 1101. Lead Responsibilities. In addition to the applicable responsibilities covered in Parts 1 and 2, the Attorney General of the United States shall:

(1)   Provide legal advice to the President and the heads of Federal departments and agencies and their successors regarding national security emergency powers, plans, and authorities;

(2)   Coordinate Federal Government domestic law enforcement activities related to national security emergency preparedness, including Federal law enforcement liaison with, and assistance to, State and local governments;

(3)   Coordinate contingency planning for national security emergency law enforcement activities that are beyond the capabilities of State and local agencies;

(4)   Develop national security emergency plans for regulation of immigration, regulation of nationals of enemy countries, and plans to implement laws for the control of persons entering or leaving the United States;

(5)   Develop plans and procedures for the custody and protection of prisoners and the use of Federal penal and correctional institutions and resources during national security emergencies;

(6)   Provide information and assistance to the Federal Judicial branch and the Federal Legislative branch concerning law enforcement, continuity of government, and the exercise of legal authority during national security emergencies;

(7)   Develop intergovernmental and interagency law enforcement plans and counterterrorism programs to interdict and respond to terrorism incidents in the United States that may result in national security emergency or that occur during such an emergency;

(8)   Develop intergovernmental and interagency law enforcement plans to respond to civil disturbances that may result in a national security emergency or that occur during such an emergency.

Section 1102. Support Responsibilities. The Attorney General of the United States shall:

(1)   Assist the heads of Federal departments and agencies, State and local governments, and the private sector in the development of plans to physically protect essential resources and facilities;

(2)   Support the Secretaries of State and the Treasury in plans for the protection of international organizations and foreign diplomatic, consular, and other official personnel, property, and other assets within the jurisdiction of the United States;

(3)   Support the Secretary of the Treasury in developing plans to control the movement of property entering and leaving the United States;

(4)   Support the heads of other Federal departments and agencies and State and local governments in developing programs and plans for identifying fatalities and reuniting families in national security emergencies;

(5)   Support the intelligence community in the planning of its counterintelligence and counterterrorism programs.

PART 12 – DEPARTMENT OF LABOR

Section 1201. Lead Responsibilities.   In addition to the applicable responsibilities covered in Parts 1 and 2, the Secretary of Labor shall:

(1)   Develop plans and issue guidance to ensure effective use of civilian workforce resources during national security emergencies. Such plans shall include, but not necessarily be limited to:

(a)   Priorities and allocations, recruitment, referral, training, employment stabilization including appeals procedures, use assessment, and determination of critical skill categories; and
(b)   Programs for increasing the availability of critical workforce skills and occupations;

(2)   In consultation with the Secretary of the Treasury, develop plans and procedures for wage, salary, and benefit costs stabilization during national security emergencies;

(3)   Develop plans and procedures for protecting and providing incentives for the civilian labor force during national security emergencies;

(4)   In consultation with other appropriate government agencies and private entities, develop plans and procedures for effective labor-management relations during national security emergencies.

Section 1202. Support Responsibilities.   The Secretary of Labor shall:

(1)   Support planning by the Secretary of Defense and the private sector for the provision of human resources to critical defense industries during national security emergencies;

(2)   Support planning by the Secretary of Defense and the Director of Selective Service for the institution of conscription in national security emergencies.

PART 13 – DEPARTMENT OF STATE

Section 1301. Lead Responsibilities.   In addition to the applicable responsibilities covered in Parts 1 and 2, the Secretary of State shall:

(1)   Provide overall foreign policy coordination in the formulation and execution of continuity of government and other national security emergency preparedness activities that affect foreign relations;

(2)   Prepare to carry out Department of State responsibilities in the conduct of the foreign relations of the United States during national security emergencies, under the direction of the President and in consultation with the heads of other appropriate Federal departments and agencies, including, but not limited to:

(a)   Formulation and implementation of foreign policy and negotiation regarding contingency and post-emergency plans, intergovernmental agreements, and arrangements with United States' allies;

(b)   Formulation, negotiation, and execution of policy affecting the relationships of the United States with neutral states;

(c) Formulation and execution of political strategy toward hostile or enemy states;

(d) Conduct of mutual assistance activities;

(e) Provision of foreign assistance, including continuous supervision and general direction of authorized economic and military assistance programs;

(f) Protection or evacuation of United States citizens and nationals abroad and safeguarding their property abroad, in consultation with the Secretaries of Defense and Health and Human Services;

(g) Protection of international organizations and foreign diplomatic, consular, and other official personnel and property, or other assets, in the United States, in coordination with the Attorney General and the Secretary of the Treasury;

(h) Formulation of policies and provisions for assistance to displaced persons and refugees abroad;

(i) Maintenance of diplomatic and consular representation abroad; and

(j) Reporting of and advising on conditions overseas that bear upon national security emergencies.

Section 1302. Support Responsibilities. The Secretary of State shall:

(1) Assist appropriate agencies in developing planning assumptions concerning accessibility of foreign sources of supply;

(2) Support the Secretary of the Treasury, in consultation, as appropriate, with the Secretaries of Commerce and Defense, in the formulation and execution of economic measures with respect to other nations;

(3) Support the Secretary of Energy in international liaison activities pertaining to nuclear materials facilities;

(4) Support the Director of the Federal Emergency Management Agency in the coordination and integration of United States policy regarding the formulation and implementation of civil emergency resources and preparedness planning;

(5) Assist the Attorney General of the United States in the formulation of national security emergency plans for the control of persons entering or leaving the United States.

PART 14 – DEPARTMENT OF TRANSPORTATION

Section 1401. Lead Responsibilities. In addition to the applicable responsibilities covered in Parts 1 and 2, the Secretary of Transportation shall:

(1) Develop plans to promulgate and manage overall national policies, programs, procedures, and systems to meet essential civil and military transportation needs in national security emergencies;

(2) Be prepared to provide direction to all modes of civil transportation in national security emergencies, including air, surface, water, pipelines, and public storage and warehousing, to the extent such responsibility is vested in the Secretary of Transportation. This direction may include:

(a) Implementation of priorities for all transportation resource requirements for service, equipment, facilities, and systems;

(b) Allocation of transportation resource capacity; and

(c) Emergency management and control of civil transportation resources and systems, including privately owned automobiles, urban mass transit, intermodal transportation systems, the National Railroad Passenger Corporation and the St. Lawrence Seaway Development Corporation;

(3) Develop plans to provide for the smooth transition of the Coast Guard as a service to the Department of the Navy during national security emergencies. These plans shall be compatible with the Department of Defense planning systems, especially in the areas of port security and military readiness;

(4) In coordination with the Secretary of State and the

Director of the Federal Emergency Management Agency, represent the United States in transportation-related international (including NATO and allied) civil emergency preparedness planning and related activities;

(5) Coordinate with State and local highway agencies in the management of all Federal, State, city, local, and other highways, roads, streets, bridges, tunnels, and publicly owned highway maintenance equipment to assure efficient and safe use of road space during national security emergencies;

(6) Develop plans and procedures in consultation with appropriate agency officials for maritime and port safety, law enforcement, and security over, upon, and under the high seas and waters subject to the jurisdiction of the United States to assure operational readiness for national security emergency functions;

(7) Develop plans for the emergency operation of U.S. ports and facilities, use of shipping resources (U.S. and others), provision of government war risks insurance, and emergency construction of merchant ships for military and civil use;

(8) Develop plans for emergency management and control of the National Airspace System, including provision of war risk insurance and for transfer of the Federal Aviation Administration, in the event of war, to the Department of Defense;

(9) Coordinate the Interstate Commerce Commission's development of plans and preparedness programs for the reduction of vulnerability, maintenance, restoration, and operation of privately owned railroads, motor carriers, inland waterway transportation systems, and public storage facilities and services in national security emergencies.

Section 1402. Support Responsibilities. The Secretary of Transportation shall coordinate with the Secretary of Energy in the planning and management of transportation resources involved in the bulk movement of energy materials.

PART 15 – DEPARTMENT OF THE TREASURY

Section 1501. Lead Responsibilities. In addition to the applicable responsibilities covered in Parts 1 and 2, the Secretary of the Treasury shall:

(1)   Develop plans to maintain stable economic conditions and a market economy during national security emergencies; emphasize measures to minimize inflation and disruptions; and, minimize reliance on direct controls of the monetary, credit, and financial systems. These plans will include provisions for:

- (a)   Increasing capabilities to minimize economic dislocations by carrying out appropriate fiscal, monetary, and regulatory policies and reducing susceptibility to manipulated economic pressures;
- (b)   Providing the Federal Government with efficient and equitable financing sources and payment mechanisms;
- (c)   Providing fiscal authorities with adequate legal authority to meet resource requirements;
- (d)   Developing, in consultation with the Board of Governors of the Federal Reserve System, and in cooperation with the Board of Directors of the Federal Deposit Insurance Corporation, the Federal Home Loan Bank Board, the National Credit Union Administration Board, the Farm Credit Administration Board and other financial institutions, plans for the continued or resumed operation and liquidity of banks, savings and loans, credit unions, and farm credit institutions, measures for the reestablishment of evidence of assets or liabilities, and provisions for currency withdrawals and deposit insurance;

(2)   Provide for the protection of United States financial resources including currency and coin production and redemption facilities, Federal check disbursement facilities, and precious monetary metals;

(3)   Provide for the preservation of, and facilitate emergency operations of, public and private financial institution systems, and provide for their restoration during or after national security emergencies;

(4)   Provide, in coordination with the Secretary of State, for participation in bilateral and multilateral financial arrangements with foreign governments;

(5) Maintain the Federal Government accounting and financial reporting system in national security emergencies;

(6) Develop plans to protect the President, the Vice President, other officers in the order of presidential succession, and other persons designated by the President;

(7) Develop plans for restoration of the economy following an attack; for the development of emergency monetary, credit, and Federal benefit payment programs of those Federal departments and agencies that have responsibilities dependent on the policies or capabilities of the Department of the Treasury; and for the implementation of national policy on sharing war losses;

(8) Develop plans for initiating tax changes, waiving regulations, and, in conjunction with the Secretary of Commerce or other guaranteeing agency, granting or guaranteeing loans for the expansion of industrial capacity, the development of technological processes, or the production or acquisition of essential materials;

(9) Develop plans, in coordination with the heads of other appropriate Federal departments and agencies, to acquire emergency imports, make foreign barter arrangements, or otherwise provide for essential material from foreign sources using, as appropriate, the resources of the Export-Import Bank or resources available to the Bank;

(10) Develop plans for encouraging capital inflow and discouraging the flight of capital from the United States and, in coordination with the Secretary of State, for the seizure and administration of assets of enemy aliens during national security emergencies;

(11) Develop plans, in consultation with the heads of appropriate Federal departments and agencies, to regulate financial and commercial transactions with other countries;

(12) Develop plans, in coordination with the Secretary of Commerce and the Attorney General of the United States, to control the movement of property entering or leaving the United States;

(13) Cooperate and consult with the Chairman of the Securities and Exchange Commission, the Chairman of the Federal

Reserve Board, the Chairman of the Commodities Futures Trading Commission in the development of emergency financial control plans and regulations for trading of stocks and commodities, and in the development of plans for the maintenance and restoration of stable and orderly markets;

(14) Develop plans, in coordination with the Secretary of State, for the formulation and execution of economic measures with respect to other nations in national security emergencies.

Section 1502. Support Responsibilities. The Secretary of the Treasury shall:

(1) Cooperate with the Attorney General of the United States on law enforcement activities, including the control of people entering and leaving the United States;

(2) Support the Secretary of Labor in developing plans and procedures for wage, salary, and benefit costs stabilization;

(3) Support the Secretary of State in plans for the protection of international organizations and foreign diplomatic, consular, and other official personnel and property or other assets in the United States.

PART 16 – ENVIRONMENTAL PROTECTION AGENCY

Section 1601. Lead Responsibilities. In addition to the applicable responsibilities covered in Parts 1 and 2, the Administrator of the Environmental Protection Agency shall:

(1) Develop Federal plans and foster development of State and local plans designed to prevent or minimize the ecological impact of hazardous agents (biological, chemical, or radiological) introduced into the environment in national security emergencies;

(2) Develop, for national security emergencies, guidance on acceptable emergency levels of nuclear radiation, assist in determining acceptable levels of biological agents, and help to provide detection and identification of chemical agents;

(3) Develop, in coordination with the Secretary of Defense, plans to assure the provision of potable water supplies to meet community needs under national security emergency conditions,

including claimancy for materials and equipment for public water systems.

Section 1602. Support Responsibilities. The Administrator of the Environmental Protection Agency shall:

(1) Assist the heads of other Federal agencies that are responsible for developing plans for the detection, reporting, assessment, protection against, and reduction of effects of hazardous agents introduced into the environment;

(2) Advise the heads of Federal departments and agencies regarding procedures for assuring compliance with environmental restrictions and for expeditious review of requests for essential waivers.

PART 17 – FEDERAL EMERGENCY MANAGEMENT AGENCY

Section 1701. Lead Responsibilities. In addition to the applicable responsibilities covered in Parts 1 and 2, the Director of the Federal Emergency Management Agency shall:

(1) Coordinate and support the initiation, development, and implementation of national security emergency preparedness programs and plans among Federal departments and agencies;

(2) Coordinate the development and implementation of plans for the operation and continuity of essential domestic emergency functions of the Federal Government during national security emergencies;

(3) Coordinate the development of plans, in cooperation with the Secretary of Defense, for mutual civil-military support during national security emergencies;

(4) Guide and assist State and local governments and private sector organizations in achieving preparedness for national security emergencies, including the development of plans and procedures for assuring continuity of government, and support planning for prompt and coordinated Federal assistance to States and localities in responding to national security emergencies;

(5) Provide the President a periodic assessment of Federal, State, and local capabilities to respond to national security emergencies;

(6)   Coordinate the implementation of policies and programs for efficient mobilization of Federal, State, local and private resources in response to national security emergencies;

(7)   Develop and coordinate with all appropriate agencies civil defense programs to enhance Federal, State, local, and private sector capabilities for national security emergency crisis management, population protection, and recovery in the event of an attack on the United States;

(8)   Develop and support public information, education, and training programs to assist Federal, State, and local government and private sector entities in planning for and implementing national security emergency preparedness programs;

(9)   Coordinate among the heads of Federal, State, and local agencies the planning, conduct, and evaluation of national security emergency exercises;

(10)   With the assistance of the heads of other appropriate Federal departments and agencies, develop and maintain capabilities to assess actual attack damage and residual recovery capabilities as well as capabilities to estimate the effects of potential attacks on the Nation;

(11)   Provide guidance to the heads of Federal departments and agencies on the appropriate use of defense production authorities, including resource claimancy, in order to improve the capability of industry and infrastructure systems to meet national security emergency needs;

(12)   Assist the Secretary of State in coordinating the formulation and implementation of United States policy for NATO and other allied civil emergency planning, including the provision of:

(a)   advice and assistance to the departments and agencies in alliance civil emergency planning matters;

(b)   support to the United States mission to NATO in the conduct of day-to-day civil emergency planning activities; and

(c)   support facilities for NATO Civil Wartime Agencies in cooperation with the Departments of Agriculture, Commerce, Energy, State, and Transportation.

Section 1702. Support Responsibilities. The Director of the Federal Emergency Management Agency shall:

(1)   Support the heads of other Federal departments and agencies in preparing plans and programs to discharge their national security emergency preparedness responsibilities, including, but not limited to, such programs as mobilization preparedness, continuity of government planning, and continuance of industry and infrastructure functions essential to national security;

(2)   Support the Secretary of Energy, the Secretary of Defense, and the Members of the Nuclear Regulatory Commission in developing, analyzing, mitigating, and responding to emergencies related to nuclear weapons, materials, and devices, including mobile and fixed nuclear facilities, by providing inter alia, off-site coordination;

(3)   Support the Administrator of General Services in efforts to promote a government-wide program with respect to Federal buildings and installations to minimize the effects of attack and establish shelter management organizations.

PART 18 – GENERAL SERVICES ADMINISTRATION

Section 1801. Lead Responsibilities.   In addition to the applicable responsibilities covered in Parts 1 and 2, the Administrator of General Services shall:

(1)   Develop national security emergency plans and procedures for the operation, maintenance, and protection of federally owned and occupied buildings managed by the General Services Administration, and for the construction, alteration, and repair of such buildings;

(2)   Develop national security emergency operating procedures for the control, acquisition, leasing, assignment, and priority of occupancy of real property by the Federal Government, and by State and local governments acting as agents of the Federal Government, except for the military facilities and facilities with

special nuclear materials within the jurisdiction of the Departments of Defense and Energy;

(3) Develop national security emergency operational plans and procedures for the use of public utility services (other than telecommunications services) by Federal departments and agencies, except for Department of Energy-operated facilities;

(4) Develop plans and operating procedures of government-wide supply programs to meet the requirements of Federal departments and agencies during national security emergencies;

(5) Develop plans and operating procedures for the use, in national security emergencies, of excess and surplus real and personal property by Federal, State, and local governmental entities;

(6) Develop plans, in coordination with the Director of the Federal Emergency Management Agency, with respect to Federal buildings and installations, to minimize the effects of attack and establish shelter management organizations.

Section 1802. Support Responsibility.   The Administrator of General Services shall develop plans to assist Federal departments and agencies in operation and maintenance of essential automated information processing facilities during national security emergencies.

PART 19 – NATIONAL AERONAUTICS AND SPACE ADMINISTRATION

Section 1901. Lead Responsibility.   In addition to the applicable responsibilities covered in Parts 1 and 2, the Administrator of the National Aeronautics and Space Administration shall coordinate with the Secretary of Defense to prepare for the use, maintenance, and development of technologically advanced aerospace and aeronautical-related systems, equipment, and methodologies applicable to national security emergencies.

PART 20 – NATIONAL ARCHIVES AND RECORDS ADMINISTRATION

Section 2001. Lead Responsibilities.   In addition to the applicable responsibilities covered in Parts 1 and 2, the Archivist of the United States shall:

(1) Develop procedures for publication during national security emergencies of the Federal Register for as broad public dissemination as is practicable of presidential proclamations and Executive orders, Federal administrative regulations, Federal emergency notices and actions, and Acts of Congress;

(2) Develop emergency procedures for providing instructions and advice on the handling and preservation of records critical to the operation of the Federal government in national security emergencies.

PART 21 – NUCLEAR REGULATORY COMMISSION

Section 2101. Lead Responsibilities.   In addition to the applicable responsibilities covered in Parts 1 and 2, the Members of the Nuclear Regulatory Commission shall:

(1) Promote the development and maintenance of national security emergency preparedness programs through security and safeguards programs by licensed facilities and activities;

(2) Develop plans to suspend any licenses granted by the Commission; to order the operations of any facility licensed under Section 103 or 104; Atomic Energy Act of 1954, as amended (42 U.S.C. 2133 or 2134); to order the entry into any plant or facility in order to recapture special nuclear material as determined under Subsection (3) below; and operate such facilities;

(3) Recapture or authorize recapture of special nuclear materials from licensees where necessary to assure the use, preservation, or safeguarding of such materials for the common defense and security, as determined by the Commission or as requested by the Secretary of Energy.

Section 2102. Support Responsibilities. The Members of the Nuclear Regulatory Commission shall:

(1) Assist the Secretary of Energy in assessing damage to Commission-licensed facilities, identifying useable facilities, and estimating the time and actions necessary to restart inoperative facilities;

(2) Provide advice and technical assistance to Federal, State, and local officials and private sector organizations regarding radiation hazards and protective actions in national security emergencies.

PART 22 – OFFICE OF PERSONNEL MANAGEMENT

Section 2201. Lead Responsibilities. In addition to the applicable responsibilities covered in Parts 1 and 2, the Director of the Office of Personnel Management shall:

(1) Prepare plans to administer the Federal civilian personnel system in national security emergencies, including plans and procedures for the rapid mobilization and reduction of an emergency Federal workforce;

(2) Develop national security emergency workforce policies for Federal civilian personnel;

(3) Develop plans to accommodate the surge of Federal personnel security background and pre-employment investigations during national security emergencies.

Section 2202. Support Responsibilities. The Director of the Office of Personnel Management shall:

(1) Assist the heads of other Federal departments and agencies with personnel management and staffing in national security emergencies, including facilitating transfers between agencies of employees with critical skills;

(2) In consultation with the Secretary of Defense and the Director of the Selective Service, develop plans and procedures for a system to control any conscription of Federal civilian employees during national security emergencies.

PART 23 – SELECTIVE SERVICE SYSTEM

Section 2301. Lead Responsibilities.   In addition to the applicable responsibilities covered in Parts 1 and 2, the Director of Selective Service shall:

(1)   Develop plans to provide by induction, as authorized by law, personnel that would be required by the armed forces during national security emergencies;

(2)   Develop plans for implementing an alternative service program.

PART 24 – TENNESSEE VALLEY AUTHORITY

Section 2401. Lead Responsibility.   In addition to the applicable responsibilities covered in Parts 1 and 2, the Board of Directors of the Tennessee Valley Authority shall develop plans and maintain river control operations for the prevention or control of floods affecting the Tennessee River System during national security emergencies.

Section 2402. Support Responsibilities.   The Board of Directors of the Tennessee Valley Authority shall:

(1)   Assist the Secretary of Energy in the development of plans for the integration of the Tennessee Valley Authority power system into nationwide national security emergency programs;

(2)   Assist the Secretaries of Defense, Interior, and Transportation and the Chairman of the Interstate Commerce Commission in the development of plans for operation and maintenance of inland waterway transportation in the Tennessee River System during national security emergencies.

PART 25 – UNITED STATES INFORMATION AGENCY

Section 2501. Lead Responsibilities.   In addition to the applicable responsibilities covered in Parts 1 and 2, the Director of the United States Information Agency shall:

(1)   Plan for the implementation of information programs to promote an understanding abroad of the status of national security emergencies within the United States;

(2)   In coordination with the Secretary of State's exercise of telecommunications functions affecting United States diplomatic missions and consular offices overseas, maintain the capability to provide television and simultaneous direct radio broadcasting in major languages to all areas of the world, and the capability to provide wireless file to all United States embassies during national security emergencies.

Section 2502. Support Responsibility. The Director of the United States Information Agency shall assist the heads of other Federal departments and agencies in planning for the use of media resources and foreign public information programs during national security emergencies.

PART 26 – UNITED STATES POSTAL SERVICE

Section 2601. Lead Responsibility.   In addition to the applicable responsibilities covered in Parts 1 and 2, the Postmaster General shall prepare plans and programs to provide essential postal services during national security emergencies.

Section 2602. Support Responsibilities. The Postmaster General shall:

(1)   Develop plans to assist the Attorney General of the United States in the registration of nationals of enemy countries residing in the United States;

(2)   Develop plans to assist the Secretary of Health and Human Services in registering displaced persons and families;

(3)   Develop plans to assist the heads of other Federal departments and agencies in locating and leasing privately owned property for Federal use during national security emergencies.

PART 27 – VETERANS ADMINISTRATION

Section 2701. Lead Responsibilities.   In addition to the applicable responsibilities covered in Parts 1 and 2, the Administrator of Veterans' Affairs shall:

(1)   Develop plans for provision of emergency health care services to veteran beneficiaries in Veterans' Administration medical facilities, to active duty military personnel and, as resources permit, to civilians in communities affected by national security emergencies;

(2)   Develop plans for mortuary services for eligible veterans, and advise on methods for interment of the dead during national security emergencies.

Section 2702. Support Responsibilities.   The Administrator of Veterans' Affairs shall:

(1)   Assist the Secretary of Health and Human Services in promoting the development of State and local plans for the provision of medical services in national security emergencies, and develop appropriate plans to support such State and local plans;

(2)   Assist the Secretary of Health and Human Services in developing national plans to set priorities and allocate medical resources among civilian and military claimants.

PART 28 – OFFICE OF MANAGEMENT AND BUDGET

Section 2801.   In addition to the applicable responsibilities covered in Parts 1 and 2, the Director of the Office of Management and Budget shall prepare plans and programs to maintain its functions during national security emergencies. In connection with these functions, the Director of the Office of Management and Budget shall:

(1)   Develop plans to ensure the preparation, clearance, and coordination of proposed Executive orders and proclamations;

(2)   Prepare plans to ensure the preparation, supervision, and control of the budget and the formulation of the fiscal program of the Government;

(3)   Develop plans to coordinate and communicate Executive branch views to the Congress regarding legislation and testimony by Executive branch officials;

(4)   Develop plans for keeping the President informed of the

activities of government agencies, continuing the Office of Management and Budget's management functions, and maintaining presidential supervision and direction with respect to legislation and regulations in national security emergencies.

PART 29 – GENERAL

Section 2901. Executive Order Nos. 10421 and 11490, as amended, are hereby revoked. This Order shall be effective immediately.

Ronald Reagan

The White House

November 18, 1988

Filed with the Office of the Federal Register, 1:08 pm, November 21, 1988.

SELECTED BIBLIOGRAPHY

Howard Aldrich, *Organizations and Environments* (New York: Prentice-Hall, 1979).

Francis A. Allen, *The Crimes of Politics: Political Dimensions of Criminal Justice* (Cambridge, Mass.: Harvard University Press, 1974).

Yonah Alexander and Allan S. Nanes, eds. *Legislative Responses to Terrorism* (Boston: M. Nijhoff, 1986).

Yonah Alexander and Kenneth A. Myers, eds., *Terrorism in Europe* (New York: St. Martin's Press; London: Croom Helm Ltd. Publishers, 1982).

Yonah Alexander, David Carleton, and Paul Wilkinson, eds., *Terrorism: Theory and Practice* (Boulder, Colo.: Westview Press, 1979).

Yonah Alexander, ed., *International Terrorism: National, Regional, and Global Perspectives* (New York: Praeger, 1976).

American Red Cross, *Disaster Relief Program* (Washington, DC: ARC, 1975).

American Red Cross, *Hurricane Action* (Washington, DC: ARC, 1975).

William A. Anderson, *Local Civil Defense in Natural Disaster* (Washington, DC: Office of Civil Defense, Disaster Research Center Report No. 7, 1969).

Terrill E. Arnold, *The Violence Formula: Why People Lend Sympathy and*

Support to Terrorism (Lexington, Mass.: Lexington Books, 1988).

Earl T. Baker and Tae Gordon McPhie, *Land Use Management and Regulation in Hazardous Areas* (Boulder, Colorado: University of Colorado, IBS#6, 1975).

George W. Baker and Dwight W. Chapman, eds., *Man and Society in Disaster* (New York: Basic Books, 1962).

Mohammed el Barakei, *Model Rules for Disaster Relief Operations* (New York: UN Institute for Training and Research Policy and Efficacy Studies No. 8, 1982).

Michael Baram, *Alternatives to Regulation: Managing Risks to Health, Safety and the Environment* (Lexington,Mass.: Lexington Books, 1981).

A. Barton, *Communities in Disaster* (New York: Doubleday, 1970).

J. Bowyer Bell, *A Time of Terror: How Democratic Societies Respond to Revolutionary Violence* (New York: Basic Books, 1978).

Allen P. Bristow, *Police Disaster Operations* (Springfield, Ill:Charles C. Thomas Publishers, 1972).

Ian Burton, Robert W. Kates, and Gilbert F. White, *The Environment as Hazard* (New York: Oxford University Press, 1978).

Michael T. Charles and John Kim, eds., *Emergency Management* (Springfield, Ill.: Charles C. Thomas Publishers, 1988).

Bruce B. Clary, "The Evolution and Structure of Natural Hazards Policies," *Public Administration Review* (Special Issue, 1985): 20-28.

Richard Clutterbuck, *Guerrillas and Terrorists* (London: Faber and Faber, Ltd., 1977).

Richard Clutterbuck, *Living with Terrorism*(New Rochelle, NY: Arlington House Publishers, 1975).

Raquel E. Cohen and Frederick L. Ahearn, Jr., *Handbook for Mental Health Care of Disaster Victims* (Baltimore: Johns Hopkins University Press, 1980).

Louise K. Comfort, ed., *Managing Disaster: Strategies and Policy Perspectives* (Durham, NC: Duke University Press, 1988).

Council of State Governments, *Comprehensive Emergency Preparedness Planning in State Government* (Lexington, Ky: CSG, 1976).

Council of State Governments, *The States and Natural Hazards* (Lexington, Ky: CSG, 1979).

Martha Crenshaw, ed., *Terrorism, Legitimacy, and Power* (Middletown, Conn.: Wesleyan University Press, 1983).

Brian Crozier, *Transnational Terrorism*(Gaithersburg, Md.: International Association of Chiefs of Police, 1974).

Douglas Dacy and Howard Kunreuther, *Economics of Disasters: Implications for Federal Policy* (New York: Free Press, 1979).

Thomas M. Dietz and Robert W. Rycroft, *The Risk Professionals* (New York: Russell Sage Foundation, 1987).

Christopher Dobson and Ronald Payne, *The Never-Ending War: Terrorism in the 1980's* (New York: Facts on File, 1987).

Joseph D. Douglas, Jr., and Neil C. Livingstone, *America the Vulnerable: The Threat of Chemical and Biological Warfare* (Lexington, Mass.: Lexington Books, 1987).

Christopher M. Douty, *The Economics of Disasters: The 1906 San Francisco Catastrophe* (New York: Arno Press, 1977).

Thomas E. Drabek, *The Professional Emergency Manager: Structures and Strategies for Success* (Boulder, Colo.: University of Colorado, Institute of Behavioral Science, Program on Environment and Behavior Monograph #44, 1987).

Thomas E. Drabek, Harrett Tansminga, Thomas Kilijanik, and Christopher Adams, *Managing Multiorganizational Emergency Responses* (Boulder, Colorado: Institute of Behavioral Sciences, Publication No. 6, University of Colorado, 1981).

Thomas Drabek, Alvin H. Mushkatel, and Thomas S. Kilijanik, *Earthquake Mitigation Policy: The Experience of Two States* (Boulder, Colorado: Institute of Behavioral Sciences, Publication No. 37, University of Colorado, 1983).

Yehezkel Dror, "Terrorism as a Challenge to the Democratic Capacity to Govern," pp. 65-90 in *Terrorism, Legitimacy, and Power*, edited by Martha Crenshaw (Middletown, Conn.: Wesleyan University Press, 1983).

Russell R. Dynes, *Organized Behavior in Disaster*(Lexington, Mass.: Lexington Books, 1970).

Alona E. Evans and John F. Murphy, eds., *Legal Aspects of International Terrorism* (Lexington, Mass.: Lexington Books, 1978).

Ernest Evans, *Calling a Truce to Terror: The American Response to International Terrorism* (Westport, Conn.: Greenwood Press, 1979).

Federal Emergency Management Agency, *Integrated Emergency Management System: Mitigation Program Development Guidance*, Washington, DC: FEMA-112, March 1987.

Federal Emergency Management Agency, *Hazards Analysis for Emergency Management*, Washington, DC: FEMA, CPG-1-101, September 1983.

Federal Emergency Management Agency, *Integrated Emergency Manage-

ment System: Process Overview, Washington, DC: FEMA, CPG 1-100, September 1983.

Federal Emergency Management Agency, *An Assessment of the Consequences and Preparations for a Catastrophic California Earthquake: Findings and Actions Taken*, Washington, DC: FEMA, M&R-2, November 1980.

Federal Emergency Management Agency, *Questions and Answers on Crisis Relocation*, Washington, DC: FEMA, P&P-4, October 1980.

Federal Emergency Management Agency, *Civil Defense and the Public: An Overview of Public Attitudes Studies*, Washington, DC: FEMA, MP-62, September 1979.

Edward D. Feigenbaum and Mark L. Ford, *Emergency Management in the States* (Lexington, Ky: Council of State Governments, 1984).

Harold D. Foster, *Disaster Planning: Preservation of Life and Property*(New York: Springer-Verlag, 1980).

H. Paul Friesema, ed., *Aftermath: Communities After Natural Disasters* (Beverly Hills, Calif.: Sage Publications, 1979).

Noemi Gal-Or, *International Cooperation to Suppress Terrorism* (New York: St. Martin's Press, 1985).

David Galula, *Counterinsurgency Warfare: Theory and Practice* (New York: Praeger, 1964).

David R. Godschalk and David J. Brower, "Mitigation Strategies and Integrated Emergency Management," *Public Administration Review* (Special Issue, 1985): 64-71.

J. Eugene Haas, Robert W. Kates, and Martyn J. Bowden, eds., *Reconstruction Following Disaster* (Cambridge, Mass.: The MIT Press, 1977).

Richard J. Healy, *Emergency and Disaster Planning* (New York: Wiley, 1969).

Hans Josef Horchem, "Pre-Empting Terror" in *International Terrorism*, edited by Benjamin Metanyahu (Jerusalem: The Jonathan Institute, 1981).

International City Management Association and the Federal Emergency Management Agency, "How Prepared is Your Community for Its Next Emergency: A Manager's Checklist," *Local Government Emergency Management: A Practitioners' Workbook* (Handbook Series No. 3), ICMA and FEMA, 1980.

Sheila Jasanoff, *Risk Management and Political Culture*(New York: Russell Sage Foundation, 1986).

Carl Jelenko, III, and Charles F. Frey, eds., *EMS: An Overview* (Bowie,

Md.: R.J. Brady, 1976).

Brian M. Jenkins, *Combatting Terrorism Becomes a War*, Santa Monica, Calif.: Rand Corporation, P-6988, May 1984.

Brian M. Jenkins, *The Consequences of Nuclear Terrorism*, Santa Monica, Calif.: Rand Corporation, P-6373, August 1979.

Brian M. Jenkins, *Combatting International Terrorism: The Role of Congress*, Santa Monica, Calif.: Rand Corporation, P-5808, January 1977.

Brian M. Jenkins, *International Terrorism: A New Mode of Conflict* (Los Angeles: Crescent Publications, 1975).

Brian M. Jenkins, *High Technology Terrorism and Surrogate War: The Impact of New Technology on Low-Level Violence*, Santa Monica, Calif.: Rand Corporation, P-5339, 1975.

Will C. Kennedy, *The Police Department in Natural Disaster Operations*(Washington, DC: Office of Civil Defense, Office of the Secretary of the Army, 1969).

Frank Kitson, *Low Intensity Operations: Subversion, Insurgency, Peacekeeping* (London: Faber and Faber, 1971).

Richard W. Kobetz and H.H.A. Cooper, *Target Terrorism: Providing Protective Services* (Gaithersburg, Md.: International Association of Chiefs of Police, 1978).

Howard Kunreuther, *Recovery from Natural Disasters: Insurance or Federal Aid?* (Washington, DC: American Enterprise Institute, Evaluative Studies #12, 1973).

Robert Kupperman and Darrell Trent, *Terrorism: Threat, Reality, Response* (Stanford, Calif.: Hoover Institution Press, 1979).

Walter Laqueur, *Terrorism: A Study of National and International Political Violence* (Boston: Little, Brown and Co.; London: Weidenfield and Nicolson, 1977).

Walter Laqueur, "Interpretations of Terrorism - Fact, Fiction and Political Science," *Journal of Contemporary History* 12 (January 1977): 1-42.

Jennifer Leaning and Langley Keyes, eds., *The Counterfeit Ark: Crisis Relocation for Nuclear War* (Cambridge, Mass.: Ballinger, 1984).

Vivian A. Leonard, *Police Pre-Disaster Preparation* (Springfield, Ill: Charles C. Thomas, 1973).

Juliet Lodge, ed., *Terrorism: A Challenge to the State* (New York: St. Martin's Press, 1981).

Paul Lowenthal, ed., *Preventing Nuclear Terrorism: The Report and Papers of the International Task Force on Prevention of Nuclear Terrorism* (Lexington, Mass.: Lexington Books, 1987).

Peter MacAlister-Smith, *International Humanitarian Assistance: Disaster Relief Actions in International Law and Organization* (Boston: M. Nijhoff, 1985).

David McLoughlin, "A Framework for Integrated Emergency Management," *Public Administration Review* (Special Issue, 1985): 165-172.

David C. Martin and John Walcott, *Best Laid Plans: The Inside Story of America's War Against Terrorism* (New York: Harper and Row, 1988).

Peter J. May, *Recovering from Catastrophes: Federal Disaster Relief Policy and Politics* (Westport, Conn.: Greenwood Press, 1985).

Peter J. May, "FEMA's Role in Emergency Management: Examining Recent Experience," *Public Administration Review* (Special Issue, 1985): 40-48.

Peter J. May and Walter Williams, *Disaster Policy Implementation: Managing Programs Under Shared Governance* (New York: Plenum Press, 1986).

Edward Mickolus, "Trends in Transnational Terrorism," pp. 44-73 in *International Terrorism in the Contemporary World,"* edited by Marius H. Livingston (Westport, Conn.: Greenwood Press, 1978).

Edward Mickolus, "Negotiating for Hostages: A Policy Dilemma," *Orbis* 19 (Winter 1976): 1309-1325.

David L. Milbank, *International and Transnational Terrorism: Diagnosis and Prognosis*, Washington, DC: U.S. Central Intelligence Agency, PR 10030, April 1976.

Dennis Mileti, Thomas E. Drabek, and J. Eugene Haas, *Human Systems in Extreme Environments: A Sociological Perspective* (Boulder, Colorado: Institute of Behavioral Science Monograph, University of Colorado, 1975).

Eric Morris and Alan Hoe (with John Potter), *Terrorism: Threat and Response* (New York: St. Martin's Press, 1988).

John F. Murphy, *Punishing International Terrorists: The Legal Framework*(Totowa, N.J.: Rowman and Allanheld, 1985).

Alvin H. Mushkatel and Louis F. Weschler, "Emergency Management and the Intergovernmental System," *Public Administration Review* (Special Issue, 1985): 49-56.

National Governors' Association, *Emergency Strategies for Disaster Prevention and Reduction* (Washington, DC: NGA, 1980).

National Governors' Association, *Comprehensive Emergency Management Bulletin* (Washington, DC: NGA, April 1982).

National Governors' Association, *Domestic Terrorism* (Washington, DC: NGA, Emergency Preparedness Project, Center for Policy Research,

State Emergency Management Series, 1978).

National Research Council, Commission of Engineering and Technical Systems, Advisory Board of the Built Environment, *Multiple Hazard Mitigation* (Washington, DC: National Academy Press, 1983).

National Research Council, *Earthquake Prediction and Public Policy*(Washington, DC: National Academy Press, 1975).

Julian Paget, *Counter-Insurgency Operations: Techniques of Guerrilla Warfare* (New York: Walker and Co., 1967).

Pan American Health Organization, *A Guide to Health Emergency Management After Natural Disasters* (Washington, DC: PAHO, 1981).

Pan American Health Organization, *Environmental Health Management After Natural Disasters* (Washington, DC: PAH0, 1982).

Howard J. Parad, H.L.P. Resnik, and Libbie G. Parad, eds., *Emergency and Disaster Management: A Mental Health Sourcebook* (Bowie, Md.: Charles Press, 1976).

Ronald W. Perry, *The Social Psychology of Civil Defense* (Lexington, Mass.: Lexington Books, 1982).

Ronald W. Perry and Alvin H. Mushkatel, *Disaster Management: Warning, Response and Community Relocation* (Westport, Conn.: Quorum Books, Greenwood Press, 1984).

Ronald W. Perry, *Comprehensive Emergency Management: Evacuating Threatened Populations* (Greenwich, Conn.: JAI Press, 1985).

William J. Petak, "Emergency Management: A Challenge for Public Administration, *Public Administration Review* (Special Issue, 1985): 3-7.

William J. Petak and Arthur A. Atkisson, *Natural Hazard Risk Assessment and Public Policy: Anticipating the Unexpected* (New York: Springer-Verlag, 1982).

Anthony C.E. Quainton, "Terrorism and Political Violence: A Permanent Challenge to Governments, pp. 52-64 in *Terrorism, Legitimacy, and Power,* edited by Martha Crenshaw (Middletown, Conn.: Wesleyan University Press, 1983).

E.L. Quarantelli and Russell R. Dynes, "Response to Social Crisis and Disaster," *Annual Review of Sociology* 3 (1977): 23-49.

E.L. Quarantelli, *Disasters: Theory and Research* (Beverly Hills, Calif.: Sage Publications, 1978).

E.L. Quarantelli, *Organizational Behavior in Disasters and Implications for Disaster Planning* (Emmitsburg, Md.:FEMA, National Emergency Training Center, Monograph Series, 1984).

David C. Rapoport, ed., *Inside Terrorist Organizations* (New York:

Columbia University Press, 1988).

Linda Richter and William L. Waugh, Jr., "Terrorism and Tourism as Logical Companions," *Tourism Management* (December 1986): 230-238.

Peter Rossi, James D. Wright, and Eleanor Weber-Burdin, *Natural Hazards and Public Choice: The State and Local Politics of Hazard Mitigation* (New York: Academic Press, 1982).

Peter Rossi et al., *Victims of the Environment: Loss from Natural Hazards in the U.S., 1970-1980* (New York: Plenum Books, 1983).

Uriel Rosenthal, Michael T. Charles, and Paul 't Hart, eds., *Coping with Crises: The Management of Disasters, Riots and Terrorism* (Springfield, Ill.: Charles C. Thomas, 1989).

Claire B. Rubin and Daniel G. Barbee, "Disaster Recovery and Hazard Mitigation: Bridging the Intergovernmental Gap," *Public Administration Review* (Special Issue, 1985): 57-63.

P.E.A. Savage, *Disasters: Hospital Planning* (New York: Pergamon Press, 1979).

Alex P. Schmid and Janny de Graaf, *Violence as Communication: Insurgent Terrorism and the Western News Media* (Beverly Hills, Calif.: Sage Publications, 1982).

Richard H. Shultz, Jr., and Stephen Sloan, eds., *Responding to the Terrorist Threat: Security and Crisis Management* (Elmsford, NY: Pergamon Press, 1980).

J.D. Simon, *Misperceiving the Terrorist Threat*, Santa Monica, Calif.: Rand Corporation, Rand Report R-3423-RC, June 1987.

Muriel Skeet, *Manual for Disaster Relief Work* (New York: Churchill Livingstone, 1977).

Stephen Sloan, *Simulating Terrorism* (Norman, Okla.: University of Oklahoma Press, 1981).

Paul Slovic, Howard Kunreuther, and Gilbert F. White, "Decision Processes, Rationality, and Adjustment to Natural Hazards," pp. 187-205 in *Natural Hazards: Local, National, Global*, edited by Gilbert F. White (New York: Oxford University Press, 1974).

Smithsonian Institute, *Directory of Disaster-Related Technology* (Washington, DC: U.S. Government Printing Office, 1975).

Lynn H. Stephens and Stephen J. Green, eds, *Disaster Assistance, Appraisal, Reform, and New Approaches* (New York: NYU Press, 1979).

Michael Stohl, ed., *The Politics of Terrorism*, Third Edition (New York and Basel: Marcel Dekker, Inc., 1988).

Michael Stohl and George A. Lopez, eds., *Government Violence and*

Repression: An Agenda for Research (Westport, Conn.: Greenwood Press, 1987).

Michael Stohl, David Carleton, and George A. Lopez, eds., *Testing Theories of State Violence and Repression* (Westport, Conn.: Greenwood Press, 1988).

Michael Stohl, David Carleton, George A. Lopez, and Stephen Samuels, "State Violation of Human Rights: Issues and Problems of Measurement," *Human Rights Quarterly* 8 (November 1986): 592-606.

Michael Stohl and George A. Lopez, eds., *The State as Terrorist: The Dynamics of Governmental Violence and Repression* (Westport, Conn.: Greenwood Press, 1984).

Richard T. Sylves and William L. Waugh, Jr., eds., *Cities and Disaster: North American Studies in Emergency Management* (Springfield, Ill.: Charles C. Thomas Publishers, 1989).

Denis Szabo and Ronald D. Crelinsten, "International Political Terrorism: A Challenge for Comparative Research," *Terrorism* 3 (1980): 341-348.

Thomas C. Thompkins, *Military Countermeasures to Terrorism in the 1980s*, Santa Monica, Calif.: Rand Corporation, N-2178-RC, August 1984.

Thomas P. Thornton, "Terror as a Weapon of Political Agitation," pp. 71-99 in *Internal War*, edited by Harry Eckstein (New York: Free Press, 1964).

Kathleen J. Tierney, *A Primer for Preparedness for Acute Chemical Emergencies* (Columbus, Ohio: Disaster Research Center, Ohio State University, 1980).

Oliver Trager, ed., *Fighting Terrorism: Negotiation or Retaliation?* (New York: Facts on File, 1986).

Darrell M. Trent, "A National Policy to Combat Terrorism," *Policy Review* 9 (Summer 1979): 41-53.

Barry A. Turner, *Man-Made Disaster* (New York: Crane Russak, 1978).

U.S. Department of State, *Patterns of Global Terrorism: 1988*, Washington, DC: Department of State, March 1989.

U.S. General Accounting Office, *Terrorism: Laws Cited Imposing Sanctions on Nations Supporting Terrorism*, Washington, DC: GAO, GAO/RCED-87-133FS, April 17, 1987.

U.S. General Accounting Office, *The Federal Emergency Management Agency's Plan for Revitalizing U.S. Civil Defense: A Review of Three Major Plan Components*, Washington, DC: GAO, NSIAD-84-11, April 16, 1984.

U.S. General Accounting Office, *Consolidation of Federal Assistance*

Resources Will Enhance the Federal-State Emergency Management Effort, Washington, DC: GAO, GGD-83-92, August 30, 1983.

U.S. General Accounting Office, *Management of the Federal Emergency Management Agency: A System Being Developed*, Washington, DC: GAO, GGD-83-9, January 6, 1983.

U.S. General Accounting Office, *States Can be Better Prepared to Respond to Disasters*, Washington, DC: GAO, CED-80-60, March 31, 1980.

U.S. House of Representatives, Committee on Science and Technology, *Information Technology for Emergency Management*, (Report prepared by the Congressional Research Service for the Subcommittee on Investigations and Oversight), 98th Congress, 2nd Session, October 9, 1984.

U.S. House of Representatives, Committee on Public Works and Transportation, *Federal Disaster Relief Program* (Report by the Subcommittee on Investigations and Review), 1978.

Eugene V. Walter, *Terror and Resistance: A Study of Political Violence with Case Studies of Some Primitive African Communities* (New York: Oxford University Press, 1969).

William L. Waugh, Jr., and Ronald J. Hy, eds., *Emergency Management Handbook: Policies and Programs* (Westport, Conn.: Greenwood Press, 1990).

William L. Waugh, Jr., and Jane P. Sweeney, eds., *Anti-Terrorism Policies: An International Comparison* (London and Brussels: Routledge, 1990).

William L. Waugh, Jr., "Emergency Management and the Capacities of State and Local Governments," in *Cities and Disaster: North American Studies in Emergency Management*, edited by Richard T. Sylves and William L. Waugh, Jr. (Springfield, Ill.: Charles C. Thomas Publishers, 1989).

William L. Waugh, Jr., "Informing Policy and Administration: A Comparative Perspective on Terrorism," *International Journal of Public Administration* 12 (January 1989).

William L. Waugh, Jr., "Integrating the Policy Models of Terrorism and Emergency Management," *Policy Studies Review* (Fall 1986): 286-300.

William L. Waugh, Jr. (1983) "The Values in Violence: The Organizational and Political Objectives of Terrorist Groups," *Conflict Quarterly* (Summer 1983): 5-19.

William L. Waugh, Jr., *International Terrorism: How Nations Respond to Terrorists - A Comparative Policy Analysis* (Chapel Hill, NC: Documentary Publications, 1982).

William H. Webster, "Fighting Terrorism in the United States," in

Terrorism: How the West Can Win, edited by Benjamin Netanyahu (New York: Farrar-Straus-Giroux, 1986).

Karl A. Western, *Epidemiological Surveillance After Natural Disaster*(Washington, DC: Pan American Health Organization, 1982).

Paul Wilkinson, *Terrorism and the Liberal State* (New York: Wiley, 1977).

Paul Wilkinson, *Political Terrorism* (London: Macmillan Press, Ltd., 1974).

Eric Willenz, "U.S. Policy on Terrorism: In Search of an Answer," *Terrorism* 9 (1987): 225-240.

Gilbert F. White, ed., *Natural Hazards: Local, National, Global* (New York: Oxford University Press, 1974).

James D. Wright and Peter H. Rossi, "The Politics of Natural Disaster: State and Local Elites," pp. 45-67 in *Social Science and Natural Hazards,* edited by James D. Wright and Peter H. Rossi (Cambridge, Mass.: Abt Books, 1981).

James D. Wright, ed., *After the Clean-Up: Long Range Effects of Natural Disasters* (Beverly Hills, Calif.: Sage Publications, 1979).

Edward Zucherman, *The Day After World War III: The U.S. Government's Plans for Surviving a Nuclear War* (New York: Viking Press, 1984).

INDEX

Abortion clinics, attacks on, 9,
114
Abu Abbas, 106
Achille Lauro, 106, 108
Acid rain, 87
Agency for Toxic Substances
and Disease Registry, 37
Air Carrier Standard Security
Program, 119
Algeria, 43
American Public Works
Association, 21
American Society for Public
Administration, 21
Amnesty International, 81, 113
"Angry violence," 46, 59, 77,
112
Anti-Hijacking Act of 1974 (PL
3-366), 119
Antiterrorism industry, 9

Anti-Terrorism Training
Assistance (Department of
State), 120
Antiterrorism units, 59, 88, 98,
109, 117, 120, 124, 125, 133,
149
Armenia, 90, 128
Arms Control and
Disarmament Agency, 109
Arms Export Control Act of
1968 (PL 90-629), 121
Atlanta, 23
Aviation, threats to, 3, 59, 67,
83, 106, 107, 118–120, 122,
125–136, 150

Bank robberies, 9
Beirut, 51, 103, 119
Belfast, 51

Biological threats, 2, 22, 88, 98,
    143, 148, 175, 186
Black September Organization,
    129
Bombings, 4, 9, 106, 118, 120
Bradish, Warren A. (U.S. Army,
    Ft. McPherson), 98
Buildings, threats to, 4
Bureau of Alcohol, Tobacco,
    and Firearms, 109
Bush, George, 101, 107

California, 6
Carter, Jimmy, 66, 101
Carter, Ambassador W. Beverly,
    130
Centers for Disease Control, 32,
    33–36, 37
Central Intelligence Agency, 10,
    102, 106, 120, 123–124
Chemical threats, 2, 175, 186
Chernobyl, 4
Civil defense, 5, 7, 20, 21, 26,
    110, 131, 142, 153, 162, 176,
    188
Civil disorder model, 43, 44,
    45–46, 62, 77, 87, 111, 112,
    116
Communications networks,
    threats to, 3, 42, 83, 98
Congo, The, 43
Congress, 195
Croatian terrorists, 128
Cuba, 3, 44, 122, 127
Cyprus, 2, 43, 123

Dams
    safety of, 27
    threats to, 4
Death squads, 125

Delta Force (U.S. Army), 109
Diplomatic personnel and
    facilities, threats to, 61, 67,
    106, 120, 122
Disaster mitigation, 4, 5, 8, 9,
    10, 11, 12, 15–16, 18, 22, 23,
    37, 41, 43, 74, 76, 77, 79,
    81, 82, 87, 89, 90, 91–93,
    117, 130, 132, 141, 143, 144,
    145, 148–149, 169
Disaster preparedness, 4, 5, 6,
    8, 9, 10, 11, 12, 15–17, 22,
    23, 37, 41, 43, 67, 76, 78,
    79, 83, 85–86, 87, 89, 90,
    91–93, 110, 116–117, 130,
    131, 141, 143, 144, 148–149,
    151, 158, 164, 166, 170, 176,
    181
Disaster Relief Act of 1950, 26
Disaster recovery, 4, 5–6, 8, 9,
    10, 11, 15–18, 22, 23, 24, 30,
    38, 41, 43, 75, 79, 89, 90–93,
    142, 143, 144, 148, 170
Disaster response, 4, 5, 8, 9, 10,
    11, 12, 15–17, 22, 23, 30, 37,
    41, 43, 66, 71, 74, 76, 77,
    78–81, 82, 83–84, 109, 123,
    133, 135, 136, 140–141, 156,
    161
Doherty, Joe, 122–123
"Domestic terrorism," 11, 103,
    106, 128
Dresden, bombing of, 42
Drug Enforcement Agency,
    104, 124

Earthquake Hazards Reduction
    Act of 1977, 27
Earthquakes, 5, 6, 27, 32, 144,
    145

Eastern Europe, 3
Egypt, 107
Emergency Support Teams, 106
Environmental Protection
    Agency, 37, 132, 166,
    186–187
Executive Order 12127 (1979),
    27
Executive Order 12472, 160
Executive Order 12656 (1988),
    107, 110, 131, 148, 157–196
Export Administration Act of
    1979 (PL 96-72), 121–122
Export-Import Bank Act of
    1945, 121
Extradition, 54, 122–123

Federal Aviation Act of 1958
    (PL 85-726), 119, 121–122
Federal Aviation
    Administration, 107, 119,
    120, 125, 130, 132, 183
Federal Civil Defense Act of
    1950, 26
Federal Bureau of Investigation,
    9, 104, 106, 108, 109, 114,
    120, 123–124, 128, 130, 132,
    133, 151
  Hostage Rescue Team, 109
  Terrorist Research and
    Analytic Center, 114
Federal Emergency
    Management Agency, 4, 12,
    20, 21, 25, 28, 29–30, 31, 32,
    37, 107, 110, 127, 130, 131,
    133, 152, 159, 160, 162, 166,
    168, 169, 172, 174, 176, 181,
    183, 187–189, 190
Federal Protective Service,
    107–108

Federal Reserve Board, 186
Flood Control Act of 1936, 26,
    27
Floods, 6
Florida, 6
Foreign Assistance Act of 1961
    (PL 87-195), 121
France, 68, 99, 119

General Accounting Office, 117,
    131, 132
General Services
    Administration, 25, 27,
    107–108, 132, 189–190
Giuffrida, Louis, 110
Great Britain, 51, 82, 123
Greece, 119
Grenada, 127

Hague Convention of 1970,
    118, 119
Hiroshima, bombing of, 4, 43,
    47
Hostage Rescue Team (FBI),
    109
Human rights, 66, 67, 75, 87,
    89, 91, 100, 113–114 (see
    also Amnesty International)
Human rights (or repressive
    violence) model, 43, 44,
    48–49, 111, 113
Hurricanes, 6, 11, 144

Immigration and Nationality
    Act of 1952, 121
Indochina, 43
Integrated Emergency Man-
    agement System (IEMS),
    4–5, 12, 29–30, 31, 37,
    73–74, 102, 144, 148–149

Intelligence gathering, 62, 79,
    124, 149, 179
Interdepartmental Group on
    Terrorism, 107
International conflict (or
    surrogate warfare) model,
    43, 44, 47, 111, 113
International Emergency
    Economic Powers Act of
    1977 (PL 95-223), 121–122
International Security and
    Development Cooperation
    Act of 1985 (PL 99-83), 119,
    121–122
"International terrorism," 2, 11,
    43, 61, 87, 100, 102–103,
    106, 133, 146
Intifada, 125
Iran-Contra scandal, 124
Irish Republican Army (IRA),
    81, 123
Iran, 44, 97, 99, 108, 109, 122,
    128, 133
Iraq, 122
Ireland, Republic of, 123
Israel, 2, 87, 99, 109, 111, 125,
    146–147

Japan, 46
Joint Chiefs of Staff
    (Department of Defense),
    106
Joint Special Operations
    Command, 106

Kidnappings, 9
Kissinger, Henry, 129–130
Ku Klux Klan, 100, 114

"Latent terrorism," 50

Latin America, 60, 120
Law enforcement model, 43,
    44, 47, 60, 62, 111, 112–113,
    114, 116, 133
Lebanon, 123, 130
Libya, 44, 108, 122, 128
London, 42, 47, 142
Los Angeles, 23

Maritime facilities, threats to,
    108, 120, 131, 182, 183
Martin, David C., 97, 101
Massachusetts, 20
Mass media, roles in terrorism,
    9, 83, 152
May, Peter J. (University of
    Washington), 7, 8, 24
Mexico, 6, 68
Montreal Convention of 1971,
    118

Nagasaki, bombing of, 4, 43
National Aeronautics and
    Space Administration, 132,
    170, 190
National Archives and Records
    Administration, 132, 191
National Association of Schools
    of Public Affairs and
    Administration, 21
National Emergencies Act of
    1976 (PL 94-412), 121
National Flood Insurance Act
    of 1968, 27
National Forest Service, 35
National Governors'
    Association, 15
National Security Agency, 106
National Security Council, 106,
    107, 158, 159, 160, 163, 164

National Security Directive 30, 106
National Security Directive 138, 124
National Weather Service, 28
Netherlands, The, 82
New Hampshire, 20
New York City, 105–106, 123, 129
Nixon, Richard M., 129
North, LTC Oliver, 106
North Atlantic Treaty Organization, 168, 183, 188
Northern Ireland (Emergency Provisions) Act of 1973, 81
Nuclear Emergency Search Teams (Department of Energy), 109
Nuclear facilities, threats to, 4, 109, 117, 118
Nuclear Regulatory Commission, 28, 36, 107, 109, 110, 132, 169, 174, 189, 191–192
Nuclear warfare, 5, 7, 83, 142, 148
Nuclear weapons, 169, 189

Occupational Safety and Health Administration, 37
Office of Management and Budget, 132, 195
Office of Personnel Management, 132, 170, 192
Office of Science and Technology, 164
"Official terrorism," 11, 113 (see Repressive terrorism and state terrorism)
Olympics, 1984, 23

Omnibus Diplomatic Security and Antiterrorism Act of 1986 (PL 99-399), 109, 121
Order, The, 114
Ozone depletion, 87

Pakistan, 108
Palestine, 43, 88, 99, 125
Pan Am Flight 103 bombing (1988), 119, 126
Philippines, 125
Ports and Waterways Safety Act of 1972, 108
Posse Comitatus (right-wing group), 114
Posse Comitatus Act (1878), 109
Power networks, threats to, 3, 4, 42, 83, 98
President, 158, 185, 187, 195
Presidential disaster declarations, 18, 132
Public health, 21, 22, 30, 32–36, 37, 86 (see Public Health Service and/or specific threats to health)
Public Health Service, 30, 32, 33–36
Public works, 21

Quainton, Ambassador Anthony C.E., 102

Radiological (nuclear) threats, 2, 22, 88, 98, 142, 143, 175, 186
Rafsanjani, Hashemi, 94
Reagan, Ronald, 97, 101, 107, 113, 124, 127, 130, 196
Red Cross, 24, 105

"Repressive terrorism," 11, 43, 66, 113 (*see* Human rights and state terrorism)
Revolution (or national liberation) model, 43, 44, 45, 51, 62, 87, 111, 112, 116
"Revolutionary terrorism," 11, 44, 45, 87, 147
Risks International, Inc., 101

Saudi Arabia, 129
Scotland, 126
Seabrook Nuclear Facility, 20
Seal Team 6 (U.S. Navy), 109, 182
Selective Service System, 132, 170, 180, 192
Soviet Union, 90
"Spillover" terrorism, 104
State terrorism, 11, 67, 68, 80
Stephens, Hugh W. (University of Houston), 108
"Subrevolutionary terrorism," 11, 59
Sudan, 120, 129
Syria, 122

Tanzania, 130
Tennessee Valley Authority, 132, 165, 173, 193
Terrorist Research and Analytic Center (FBI), 114
Thermal Neutron Analysis technologies, 119
Tokyo Convention of 1963, 118
Trade Act of 1974 (PL 93-618), 121
Trade Expansion Act of 1962 (PL 87-794), 121
Trading with the Enemy Act of

1917 (1977 Amendments, PL 95-223), 121
Transnational terrorism, 11
Transportation networks, threats to, 3, 4, 42, 83, 98, 117
TWA Hijacking (1985), 119, 124

Ulster, 51
United Kingdom (*see* Great Britain)
United Nations, 69, 120
U.S. Agency for International Development, 108
U.S. Air Force, Air War College, 100
U.S. Army
    Corps of Engineers, 27, 32
    Counterintelligence and Security Division, 98
    Delta Force, 109
U.S. Coast Guard, 182
U.S. Department of Agriculture, 132, 165–166, 174, 176, 177, 188
U.S. Department of Commerce, 25, 28, 132, 165–168, 170, 171, 177, 181, 185, 188
U.S. Department of Defense, 25, 26, 109, 132, 153, 165, 166, 167, 168–172, 173, 186, 187, 189, 190, 192, 193
U.S. Department of Education, 132, 172–173, 176
U.S. Department of Energy, 36, 107, 109, 132, 169, 170, 171, 173–175, 181, 183, 188, 189, 190, 191–192, 193
U.S. Department of Health and Human Services, 132, 166,

172, 175–176, 181, 194, 195
U.S. Department of Housing
and Urban Development,
25, 27, 132, 170, 171, 174,
176–177
U.S. Department of the Interior,
132, 165, 166, 177, 193
U.S. Department of Justice
(including the Attorney
General), 106, 120, 170,
178–179, 181, 185, 194
U.S. Department of Labor, 132,
170, 172, 179–180, 186
U.S. Department of State, 100,
103, 106, 109, 120, 132, 167,
168, 169, 171, 174, 179,
180–182, 188, 194, 195, 197
Bureau of Diplomatic
Security, 108
Office of the
Ambassador-at-Large for
Counterterrorism, 108
Office for Combatting
Terrorism, 102
Office of Security, 108
Overseas Security Advisory
Council, 126
Special Programs and Liaison
Office, 108
U.S. Department of
Transportation, 36, 37, 119,
126, 132, 167, 174, 182–183,
188, 193
U.S. Department of the
Treasury, 109, 132, 164,
167, 168, 171, 179, 181,
183–186

U.S. Information Agency, 109,
132, 193–194
U.S. Marshals Service, 107
U.S. Navy, 109, 124, 182
Seal Team 6, 109
U.S. Postal Service, 132, 194
U.S. Secret Service, 109

Venezuela, 120
Veterans Administration, 132,
194–195
Vice-President, 185
Vigilante model, 43, 44, 49, 62,
111, 113–114, 116
"Vigilante terrorism," 11, 43,
114, 147
Volcanic hazards, 22, 144

Walcott, John, 97, 101
Washington, DC, 23
Water systems, threats to, 3, 4,
42, 83, 98
Western Europe, 2, 3, 44, 46,
60, 98, 111, 112, 146, 147,
150
Willenz, Eric (Carnegie
Endowment for
International Peace), 111
Williams, Walter, 8
Winkates, James E. (USAF Air
War College), 100, 101

Yemen, People's Democratic
Republic of, 122
Younis, Fawaz, 123